D1006249

Baker's Wedding Handbook

Resources for Pastors

Paul E. Engle, Editor

A Division of Baker Book House Co
Grand Rapids, Michigan 49516

© 1994 by Paul E. Engle

Published by Baker Books
a division of Baker Publishing Group
P.O. Box 6287, Grand Rapids, MI 49516-6287
www.bakerbooks.com

Printed in the United States of America

All rights reserved. No part of this publication may be reproduced,
stored in a retrieval system, or transmitted in any form or by any
means—electronic, mechanical, photocopy, recording, or any
other—without the prior written permission of the publisher. The
only exception is brief quotations in printed reviews.

The planning charts at the back of the book may be copied for
individual use.

Library of Congress Cataloging-in-Publication Data
Baker's wedding handbook / Paul E. Engle, editor.
     p.   cm.
     ISBN 10: 0-8010-3225-3
     ISBN 978-0-8010-3225-7
     1. Marriage service.   I. Engle, Paul E
BV199.M3B35   1994
264′.5—dc20   94-3052

          13   14   15   16   22   21   20   19

With love and appreciation for Margie, my bride,
and to our parents who modeled Christian
marriage,
George and Marion Engle
and
John and Margaret Walker

Paul E. Engle is an ordained minister who has served in pastoral ministry in churches in Pennsylvania, Connecticut, Illinois, and Michigan. Dr. Engle has also taught as a visiting instructor in the practical theology departments of Trinity Evangelical Divinity School, Knox Theological Seminary, and Reformed Theological Seminary. He earned degrees from Houghton College, Wheaton Graduate School, and Westminster Theological Seminary.

Contents

Preface   7

Part 1   Traditional Wedding Ceremonies

1   Baptist   13

2   Christian and Missionary Alliance   18

3   Episcopalian   26

4   Evangelical   37

5   Lutheran   44

6   Methodist   50
  *The Free Methodist Church of North
     America   50*
  The Wesleyan Church   56

7   Presbyterian   61
  Presbyterian Church in America   61

8   Reformed   66
  Christian Reformed Church   66
  Reformed Church in America   73

Part 2   Alternate Wedding Ceremonies

9   Contemporary Weddings   87
  Option One   87
  Option Two   94

10   Service of Recognition of a Civil Marriage   100

Contents

11   A Brief Wedding Ceremony   103

12   Ceremony for a Remarriage of a Couple with Children   107

13   An Ecumenical Ceremony from the Consultation on Common Texts   115

14   Service of Renewal of Wedding Vows   121

Part 3   Resources for Wedding Ceremonies

15   Wedding Meditations   127
     Marriage Is Wonderful
       D. Stuart Briscoe   127
     O-Rings and Wedding Rings
       Bryan Chapell   133
     Closer to God, Closer to Each Other
       John Guest   142
     Wedding Gifts, David W. Wiersbe   146

16   Lighting of a Unity Candle   151

17   The Lord's Supper at a Wedding   153

18   Alternate Wedding Vows   157

19   Suggested Scripture Readings for Weddings   160

20   Wedding Prayers   162

21   Wedding Music   167

22   Planning Charts   172
     Request for a Wedding   172
     Minister's Wedding Ceremony Planning Sheet   177
     Processional and Recessional Diagrams   182

Preface

Pastors are called on to participate in myriad ministerial responsibilities. One of the highest privileges afforded a pastor is that of performing a wedding ceremony for a believing couple. Pastors have "the best seat in the house" as they preside over the ceremony standing face to face with the radiant bride and groom to unite them in Christ. Pastors are eyewitnesses and participants in one of the most momentous and sacred experiences in life. A church wedding is not just a social custom with a religious veneer, an expensive aggravation to satisfy sentimental relatives, or the pretext for having a reception. Weddings are worshipful acts celebrated in the presence of the Creator of marriage, surrounded by the assembled community. Early in church history, Tertullian (c. 160–220) wrote in his *Ad Uxorem* about the joys associated with weddings:

> How should we ever be able adequately to describe the happiness of that marriage which the Church arranges, the Sacrifice strengthens, upon

which the blessing sets a seal, at which angels are present as witnesses, and to which the Father gives his consent? For not even on earth do children marry properly and legally without their father's permission. How beautiful, then, the marriage of two Christians, two who are one in hope, one in desire, one in the way of life they follow, one in the religion they practice. They are as brother and sister, both servants of the same Master. Nothing divides them, either in flesh or in spirit. They pray together, they worship together, they fast together; instructing one another, encouraging one another, strengthening one another.

Where can pastors turn for direction in planning wedding ceremonies? Although God instituted marriage as a sacred covenant (Gen. 2:24), and although the Bible makes frequent references to marriage (forty-two times) and weddings (nineteen times), Scripture prescribes no order of ceremony for weddings. We are given the freedom to apply biblical marriage principles in planning a meaningful ceremony with sensitivity to cultural, community, family, and personal preferences and customs. Yet in North America today, wedding services and customs are in transition. The growing number of divorces and remarriages, shifting family roles, and changing societal expectations call for a rethinking of how to express unchanging biblical truths about marriage in ways that address these developments. In recent years various denominations have updated their marriage services to reflect changing preferences and to respond to calls for more gender-inclusive language. *Baker's Wedding Handbook* has been compiled with these factors in mind, drawing on updated ceremonies from ten different denominations and suggesting numerous ideas for creative variations.

How can this handbook be used?

- Experienced pastors can profit from the stimulation of being exposed to a variety of wedding customs from various denominations, especially in a day when parishioners readily cross denominational lines.

- Pastors who receive special requests—such as to conduct a service for renewal of wedding vows, for blessing of a civil ceremony, or for a remarriage—can find ideas on how to proceed.

- Pastors who would like help in putting together a wedding meditation may find it stimulating to consult the sample wedding meditations in this handbook.

- Pastors can recommend this book to couples who would like to write their own ceremony.

- Ministers may choose to photocopy the charts, found in the final chapter, to use in planning upcoming weddings.

- Church musicians looking for wedding music ideas will find helpful listings.

- Ministerial students or new pastors who face performing their first wedding and need direction will find it here.

- Seminary or Bible college teachers may find this a useful wedding manual to recommend to their students or to use in pastoral duties classes.

What a privilege to preside over a wedding ceremony! Pastors have an opportunity, with God's enabling, to set the direction for a couple and to impact the course of their entire married life. It is our privilege to address both believers and nonbelievers who attend the ceremony and to expose them to God's perspective on marriage—a perspective often unheard or distorted in the popular media. In addition, what an opportunity to be an agent of covenant renewal in the lives of those already married who are attending the service.

Having planned and conducted numerous weddings during more than twenty years of pastoral ministry, I have edited this book with the prayer that all who use it will be effective ministers in building and strengthening committed Christian marriages to the glory of God.

PART 1

Traditional
Wedding
Ceremonies

✝

1

Baptist

† Organ Prelude

† Solo

† Processional

Bride follows party holding the arm of her father or someone in his stead. The pastor(s), groom, and best man enter at the front of the church.

† Call to Worship

The Lord says, "The time is coming when I will make a new covenant with my people. The new covenant will be this: I will put my law within them and write it upon their hearts. I will be their

13

God and they will be my people" (based on Jer. 31: 31–33).

† Hymn—"Love Divine, All Loves Excelling"

† Invocation and Lord's Prayer

O Lord of life and love, of light and faith, who in Jesus Christ our Lord gave your blessing at the wedding in Cana of Galilee, be present here this day as these two come to be joined as wife and husband. Even as they have been drawn together in love for each other, now join them in a love born out of their desire to walk in your path. Through him who taught us to pray, saying, "Our Father . . ."

† Reading of Scripture—1 Corinthians 13

† Meditation or Sermon

† The Service of Matrimony

Dear friends and relatives, we are gathered here today, believing that God is present with us as we celebrate the coming together in love of this woman and this man. We remember that marriage is a time when a growing love is made public, when two people share mutual promises before God and before us. We join in our prayerful support of them as they offer themselves to each other. We celebrate their joy, their love, and their expectations. We pray for them the blessed presence of Jesus Christ, that whatever human weaknesses exist will be overcome by his forgiveness and his style of relationships.

† Declaration of Intent

To groom: _____, will you have _____ to be your wife, to live with her, respect her, and love her as God intends with the promise of faithfulness, tenderness, and helpfulness, as long as you both shall live?

Groom responds: I will, God being my helper.

To bride: _____, will you have _____ to be your husband, to live with him, respect him, and love him as God intends with the promise of faithfulness, tenderness, and helpfulness, as long as you both shall live?

Bride responds: I will, God being my helper.

Minister: Who presents this bride to us?

Father of the bride or other designated person: Her family presents her with prayerful love.
(The bride's hand is given over to the groom.)

15

† The Vows

Minister says to bride: Repeat after me:

I, _____, take you, _____, to be my husband, to live with you and to love from this time forward until death separates us. I promise to be understanding, forgiving, and seeking of your happiness as we grow together in God's grace.

Minister says to groom: Repeat after me:

I, _____, take you, _____, to be my wife, to live with you and to love from this time forward until death separates us. I promise to be understanding, forgiving, and seeking of your happiness as we grow together in God's grace.

† Presentation of the Rings

This (these) ring(s) is (are) a circle, a symbol of the never-ending love that you have promised to each other. May I remind you both that the love only endures as we grow together in Christ's love. Take it, place it on her (his) finger, and repeat after me.

The ring vow spoken by each partner in turn:

I give you this ring to wear as a sign of my promise to love and grow with you.

† Prayer

Eternal God, as the source of all life and peace, we pray that _____ and _____ may now be united in a relationship blessed by your holy presence. When they make mistakes, help them to correct them with self-giving love; when childishness creeps in, help them to overcome it with maturing forgiveness; when misunderstanding enters, help them to seek out your wisdom and be united in a trusting bond that will endure for all time, through Jesus Christ our Lord. Amen.

† Pronouncement

Since _____ and _____ have exchanged promises of mutual love and have professed before those of us gathered here that they will live together as understanding, mature persons in God's sight, I now declare that they are husband and wife in the Name of the Father, Son, and Holy Spirit. Amen.

† Benediction

† Organ Recessional

From Orlando L. Tibbets, *The Minister's Handbook* (Valley Forge, Pa.: Judson Press, 1986), pp. 102–6. Used by permission of the American Baptist Board of Education and Publication.

2

Christian and Missionary Alliance

† Opening Scripture

"The Lord God said, 'It is not good for the man to be alone. I will make a helper suitable for him.' . . . Then the Lord God made a woman from the rib he had taken out of the man, and he brought her to the man. The man said, 'This is now bone of my bones and flesh of my flesh.' For this reason a man will leave his father and mother and be united to his wife, and they will become one flesh" (Gen. 2:18, 22–24).

"A woman of noble character who can find? She is worth far more than rubies. Her husband has full confidence in her and lacks nothing of value. She brings him good, not harm, all the days of her life" (Prov. 31:10–12).

A marriage has always been a joyous occasion. In Cana of Galilee it was gladdened by the presence and blessing of the Lord Jesus himself. Because God intended marriage to bring blessing and joy to your lives, let us invoke his presence as you make your covenant before him and these guests.

† Invocation

† Challenge to the Groom and Bride

To the groom: _____, the Scriptures say to the husband:

"Husbands, love your wives, just as Christ loved the church and gave himself up for her to make her holy, cleansing her by the washing with water through the word, and to present her to himself as a radiant church, without stain or wrinkle or any other blemish, but holy and blameless. In this same way, husbands ought to love their wives as their own bodies" (Eph. 5:25–28).

To the bride: And _____, the Scriptures say to the wife:

"Wives, submit to your husbands as to the Lord. For the husband is the head of the wife as Christ is the head of the church, his body, of which he is the Savior. Now as the church submits to Christ, so also wives should submit to their husbands in everything" (Eph. 5:22–24).

And to you both, the Scriptures say:

"Submit to one another out of reverence for Christ" (Eph. 5:21).

Marriage was instituted by God himself, and he performed the first marriage. When a man and a woman have chosen each other and have come to that moment when they sincerely and publicly join in this covenant for life, they lay down on the altar a holy sacrifice to God, to each other, and to humanity. The union into which you are now about to enter is the closest and most tender into which human beings can come. It is a union founded on mutual experience and affection and, to believers in the Lord Jesus Christ, it is a union in the Lord. Marriage is God's institution, intended for the happiness and welfare of humankind.

The Scriptures further say:

"Love is patient, love is kind. It does not envy, it does not boast, it is not proud. It is not rude, it is not self-seeking, it is not easily angered, it keeps no record of wrongs. Love does not delight in evil but rejoices with the truth. It always protects, always trusts, always hopes, always perseveres" (1 Cor. 13:4–7).

A union embodying such ideals is not to be entered into lightly or unadvisedly, but reverently, discreetly, soberly, and in the fear of God. Into such a union you come now to be joined.

✝ Giving of Bride

If the bride is to be given in marriage by her father or some other person, the minister will ask:

Who gives _____ to be married to _____?

The father or friend will answer: I do.

Or he may say: Her mother and I.

He will place the bride's hand in the groom's hand and then be seated.

✝ Questions of Intent

Addressing the groom, the minister will ask:

Before God and these witnesses, will you, _____, take _____, to be your wife? Will you love and comfort her, honor and keep her, and, in joy and sorrow, preserve with her this bond, holy and unbroken, until the coming of our Lord Jesus Christ, or as long as you both shall live?

The groom should be instructed in advance to respond by saying: I will.

Addressing the bride, the minister will ask:

Before God and these witnesses, will you, _____, take _____, to be your husband? Will you love and comfort him, honor and keep him, and, in joy and sorrow, preserve with him this bond, holy and unbroken, until the coming of our Lord Jesus Christ, or as long as you both shall live?

The bride should be instructed in advance to respond by saying: I will.

† Wedding Vows

Facing his bride and holding her right hand, the man will say (either from memory or following the minister phrase by phrase):

I, _____, take you, _____, to be my wife; to love you with all my heart's affection, to endow you with all my earthly possessions; to give you all the honor of my name; and to share with you the grace of my God.

Facing the groom and holding his right hand, the woman shall say (either from memory or following the minister phrase by phrase):

I, _____, take you, _____, to be my husband. Where you go I will go, and where you stay I will stay. Your people will be my people and your God my God.

† Exchange of Rings

The minister will say:

As a token of this covenant, you will now give and receive the marriage rings.

The minister will receive from the best man the bride's ring and hold it up for the couple to see.

The unbroken circle, the emblem of eternity, and the gold, the emblem of that which is least tarnished and most enduring, are to show how lasting is the pledge you have made to each other.

He hands the ring to the groom, who places it on the ring finger of the bride's left hand. The minister will receive from the maid or matron of honor the groom's ring and hold it up for the couple to see.

With these emblems of purity and endless devotion, you wed, and these marriage vows you here and now forever seal.

He hands the ring to the bride, who places it on the ring finger of the groom's left hand.

† Prayer of Dedication

The minister will announce: Let us pray.

Preferably the couple will kneel and the minister will place his hands on their shoulders as he prays.

If desired, an appropriate song may precede the prayer.

† The Pronunciation

Following the prayer, the couple will stand, if they have been kneeling, and face the minister, who will say:

Inasmuch as you, _____, and you, _____, have thus consented in holy matrimony and have witnessed the same before God and these friends, by virtue of the authority vested in me as a minister of the Word of God, and by the laws of this state, I now pronounce you husband and wife. "Therefore what God has joined together, let man not separate."

The embrace and kiss may follow.

Henceforth, you travel life's road together. Let love guide all your relationships. May Christ be the Head of your home, the Unseen Guest at every meal, and the Silent Listener to every conversation. May heaven's constant benediction crown your union with increasing joy and blessedness and unite your hearts and lives by the grace and true affection of a happy marriage.

The Lord bless you
  and keep you;
the Lord make his face shine upon you
  and be gracious to you;

the Lord turn his face toward you
and give you peace. (Num. 6:24–26)

In the Name of the Father, Son, and Holy Spirit.
Amen!

† Introduction and Recessional

This is the proper place for the pastor publicly to congratulate the couple. As they then turn for the recessional, he may introduce the new bridegroom and bride.

I present to you Mr. and Mrs. _____.
Or, I present to you _____ and _____ (last name).

From *The Pastor's Handbook* (Camp Hill, Pa.: Christian Publications, 1989), pp. 36–43. Used by permission.

3

Episcopalian

During the entrance, a hymn, Psalm, or anthem may be sung, or instrumental music may be played. Then the Celebrant, facing the people and the persons to be married, with the woman to the right and the man to the left, addresses the congregation and says:

† Dearly beloved: We have come together in the presence of God to witness and bless the joining together of this man and this woman in Holy Matrimony. The bond and covenant of marriage were established by God in creation, and our Lord Jesus Christ adorned this manner of life by his presence and first miracle at a wedding in Cana of Galilee. It signifies to us the mystery of the union between Christ and his Church, and Holy Scripture commends it to be honored among all people.

The union of husband and wife in heart, body, and mind is intended by God for their mutual joy; for the help and comfort given one another in prosperity and adversity; and, when it is God's will, for the procreation of children and their nurture in the knowledge and love of the Lord. Therefore marriage is not to be entered into unadvisedly or lightly, but reverently, deliberately, and in accordance with the purposes for which it was instituted by God.

Into this holy union _____ and _____ now come to be joined. If any of you can show just cause why they may not lawfully be married, speak now; or else for ever hold your peace.

Then the Celebrant says to the persons to be married:

I require and charge you both, here in the presence of God, that if either of you know any reason why you may not be united in marriage lawfully, and in accordance with God's Word, you do now confess it.

† The Declaration of Consent

The Celebrant says to the Woman:

_____, will you have this man to be your husband; to live together in the covenant of marriage? Will you love him, comfort him, honor and keep him, in sickness and in health; and, forsaking all others, be faithful to him as long as you both shall live?

The Woman answers: I will.

The Celebrant says to the Man:
_____, will you have this woman to be your wife; to live together in the covenant of marriage? Will you love her, comfort her, honor and keep her, in sickness and in health; and, forsaking all others, be faithful to her as long as you both shall live?

The Man answers: I will.

The Celebrant then addresses the congregation, saying:
Will all of you witnessing these promises do all in your power to uphold these two persons in their marriage?

People: We will.

If there is to be a presentation or a giving in marriage, it takes place at this time.
A hymn, Psalm, or anthem may follow.

† The Ministry of the Word

The Celebrant then says to the people:
The Lord be with you.

People: And also with you.

Let us pray.

O gracious and everliving God, you have created us male and female in your image. Look mercifully upon this man and this woman who come to you seeking your blessing, and assist them with your grace, that with true fidelity and steadfast love they may honor and keep the promises and vows they make; through Jesus Christ our Savior, who lives and reigns with you in the unity of the Holy Spirit, one God, for ever and ever. Amen.

Then one or more of the following passages from Holy Scripture is read. If there is to be a Communion, a passage from the Gospel always concludes the Readings.

Genesis 1:26–28

Genesis 2:4–9, 15–24

Song of Solomon 2:10–13; 8:6–7

1 Corinthians 13:1–13

Ephesians 3:14–19

Ephesians 5:1–2, 21–33

Colossians 3:12–17

1 John 4:7–16

Between the readings, a Psalm, hymn, or anthem may be sung or said. Appropriate Psalms are 67, 127, and 128.

When a passage from the Gospel is to be read, all stand, and the Deacon or Minister appointed says:

The Holy Gospel of our Lord Jesus Christ according to _____.

People: Glory to you, Lord Christ.

Matthew 5:1–10
Matthew 5:13–18
Matthew 7:21, 24–29
Mark 10:6–9, 13–16
John 15:9–12

After the Gospel the Reader says:
The Gospel of the Lord.

People: Praise to you, Lord Christ.

A homily or other response to the Readings may follow.

† The Marriage

The Man, facing the Woman and taking her right hand in his, says:

In the Name of God, I, _____, take you, _____, to be my wife, to have and to hold from this day forward, for better for worse, for richer for poorer, in sickness and in health, to love and to cherish, until we are parted by death. This is my solemn vow.

Then they loose their hands, and the Woman, still facing the Man, takes his right hand in hers, and says:

In the Name of God, I, _____, take you, _____, to be my husband, to have and to hold from this day forward, for better for worse, for richer for poorer, in sickness and in health, to love and to cherish, until we are parted by death. This is my solemn vow.

They loose their hands. The Priest may ask God's blessing on a ring or rings as follows:

Bless, O Lord, this ring to be a sign of the vows by which this man and this woman have bound themselves to each other; through Jesus Christ our Lord. Amen.

The giver places the ring on the ring finger of the other's hand and says:

_____, I give you this ring as a symbol of my vow, and with all that I am, and all that I have, I honor you, in the Name of the Father, and of the Son, and of the Holy Spirit.

Then the Celebrant joins the right hands of husband and wife and says:

Now that _____ and _____ have given themselves to each other by solemn vows, with the joining of hands and the giving and receiving of a ring, I pronounce that they are husband and wife, in the

Name of the Father, and of the Son, and of the Holy Spirit.

Those whom God has joined together let no one put asunder.

People: Amen.

✝ The Prayers

All standing, the Celebrant says:

Let us pray together in the words our Savior taught us.

People and Celebrant (use either version):

Our Father, who art in heaven, hallowed be thy Name, thy kingdom come, thy will be done, on earth as it is in heaven.	Our Father in heaven, hallowed be your Name, your kingdom come, your will be done, on earth as in heaven.
Give us this day our daily bread.	Give us today our daily bread.
And forgive us our trespasses, as we forgive those who trespass against us.	Forgive us our sins as we forgive those who sin against us.
And lead us not into temptation, but deliver us from evil.	Save us from the time of trial, and deliver us from evil.

For thine is the kingdom, and the power, and the glory, for ever and ever. Amen.

For the kingdom, the power, and the glory are yours, now and for ever. Amen.

✝ *If Communion is to follow, the Lord's Prayer may be omitted here.*

The Deacon or other person appointed reads the following prayers, to which the People respond, saying, Amen.

If there is not to be a Communion, one or more of the prayers may be omitted.

Let us pray.

Eternal God, creator and preserver of all life, author of salvation, and giver of all grace: look with favor upon the world you have made, and for which your Son gave his life, and especially upon this man and this woman whom you make one flesh in Holy Matrimony. Amen.

Give them wisdom and devotion in the ordering of their common life, that each may be to the other a strength in need, a counselor in perplexity, a comfort in sorrow, and a companion in joy. Amen.

Grant that their wills may be so knit together in your will, and their spirits in your Spirit, that they may grow in love and peace with you and one another all the days of their life. Amen.

Give them grace, when they hurt each other, to recognize and acknowledge their fault, and to seek each other's forgiveness and yours. Amen.

Make their life together a sign of Christ's love to this sinful and broken world, that unity may overcome estrangement, forgiveness heal guilt, and joy conquer despair. Amen.

Bestow on them, if it is your will, the gift and heritage of children, and the grace to bring them up to know you, to love you, and to serve you. Amen.

Give them such fulfillment of their mutual affection that they may reach out in love and concern for others. Amen.

Grant that all married persons who have witnessed these vows may find their lives strengthened and their loyalties confirmed. Amen.

Grant that the bonds of our common humanity, by which all your children are united one to another, and the living to the dead, may be so transformed by your grace, that your will may be done on earth as it is in heaven; where, O Father, with your Son and the Holy Spirit, you live and reign in perfect unity, now and for ever. Amen.

† The Blessing of the Marriage

The people remain standing. The husband and wife kneel, and the Priest says one of the following prayers:

Most gracious God, we give you thanks for your tender love in sending Jesus Christ to come among us, to be born of a human mother, and to make the way of the cross to be the way of life. We thank you, also, for consecrating the union of man and woman in his Name. By the power of your Holy Spirit, pour out the abundance of your blessing upon this man and this woman. Defend them from every enemy. Lead them into all peace. Let their love for each other be a seal upon their hearts, a mantle about their shoulders, and a crown upon their foreheads. Bless them in their work and in their companionship; in their sleeping and in their waking; in their joys and in their sorrows; in their life and in their death. Finally, in your mercy, bring them to that table where your saints feast for ever in your heavenly home; through Jesus Christ our Lord, who with you and the Holy Spirit lives and reigns, one God, for ever and ever. Amen.

Or this:

O God, you have so consecrated the covenant of marriage that in it is represented the spiritual unity between Christ and his Church. Send therefore your blessing upon these your servants, that they may so love, honor, and cherish each other in faithfulness and patience, in wisdom and true godliness, that their home may be a haven of blessing and peace; through Jesus Christ our

Lord, who lives and reigns with you and the Holy Spirit, one God, now and for ever. Amen.

The husband and wife still kneeling, the Priest adds this blessing:

God the Father, God the Son, God the Holy Spirit, bless, preserve, and keep you; the Lord mercifully with his favor look upon you, and fill you with all spiritual benediction and grace; that you may faithfully live together in this life, and in the age to come have life everlasting. Amen.

† The Peace

The Celebrant may say to the people:
The peace of the Lord be always with you.

People: And also with you.

The newly married couple then greet each other, after which greetings may be exchanged throughout the congregation. When Communion is not to follow, the wedding party leaves the church. A hymn, psalm, or anthem may be sung; or instrumental music may be played.

From *The Book of Common Prayer* (The Church Hymnal Corporation and The Seabury Press, 1979), pp. 423–31. Used by permission.

4

Evangelical

The wedding party may enter either during the processional music or during the singing of a congregational hymn. The woman will stand on the minister's right and the man on the left, with the other members of the wedding party on either side.

† Address to the People

Dear friends, we have gathered here in the presence of God to join this man and this woman in holy marriage, which is instituted by God, regulated by his commandments, blessed by our Lord Jesus Christ, and to be held in honor among all people. Let us therefore remember that God has established and sanctified marriage for the welfare and happiness of the human family. For this reason our Savior has declared that a man shall leave his father and mother and be joined to his wife, and the two shall become one. By his apostles he has instructed those who enter into this relationship to cherish a mutual esteem and love; to share in each other's infirmities and weaknesses; to comfort each other in sickness, trouble, and sorrow; to provide for each other and for their household; to pray for and encourage each other; and to live together as heirs of the grace of life.

† Charge to Couple and Congregation

Then, speaking to the persons being married, the minister shall say:

_____ and _____, because you have come here seeking God's blessing on your marriage, I charge you both in his presence, if either of you knows any reason why you may not be joined together, to acknowledge it now. For he who sees and knows your hearts wants nothing unresolved between you and him.

Addressing the congregation, the minister may say:

Because the blessing of God's people is also important to this union, if there are any here present who have just reason to withhold such blessing, I charge them also to make it known.

✝ Prayer

On occasion when the marriage rite is not part of a full worship service, the minister may say:

Let us pray.

Almighty God, our heavenly Father, your presence is the joy of every occasion and your favor hallows every relationship. Be especially present and gracious to these two persons, we pray, that they may truly be joined in one with your blessing. As you have brought them together in your providence, sanctify them with your Holy Spirit, giving them a new mind and heart for their life together; and grant to them, now and always, the promise of your guidance and support; through Jesus Christ our Lord. Amen.

✝ Declaration of Consent

Addressing the bridal couple, the minister will ask:

_____ *(groom)*, will you have this woman to be your wife, and will you give yourself to her in all love and honor, in all duty and service, in all faith and tenderness, to live with her and cherish her as long as you both shall live?

The groom will answer: I will.

_____ *(bride),* will you take this man to be your husband, and will you give yourself to him in all love and honor, in all duty and service, in all faith and tenderness, to live with him and cherish him as long as you both shall live?

The bride will answer: I will.

† Affirmation by the Parents

Now the minister will ask:

Will you, parents of this man and woman, give your blessing to their union? If so, answer, "I will."

The parents each respond: I will.

† Vows

Now the couple, taking each other's hands, shall say their vows:

I, _____, take you, _____, to be my wife; and I do promise and covenant, before God and these witnesses, to be your loving and faithful husband: in plenty and in want, in joy and in sorrow, in sickness and in health, as long as we both shall live.

I, _____, take you, _____, to be my husband; and I do promise and covenant, before God and these witnesses, to be your loving and faithful wife: in plenty and in want, in joy and in sorrow, in sickness and in health, as long as we both shall live.

✝ Giving and Receiving Rings

As the minister receives each ring, in turn, it is appropriate to say:

Let us pray.

Bless, O Lord, this ring, that he/she who gives it and he/she who wears it may abide in your peace and continue in your favor until their life's end.

Giving the rings, in turn, the groom and bride will say:

This ring I give you in token and pledge of our constant faith and abiding love: in the Name of the Father, and of the Son, and of the Holy Spirit. Amen.

✝ Declaration of Marriage

By the authority committed to me as a minister of the church of Jesus Christ I now declare that _____ and _____ are husband and wife, according to the ordinance of God and the laws of this state; in the Name of the Father, and of the Son, and of the Holy Spirit. Amen.

✝ Blessing

The Lord God, who created our first parents and established them in marriage, establish and sustain you, that you may find delight in each

other and grow in holy love until your life's end.
Amen.

† Prayers of Thanksgiving and Intercession

Here the couple may kneel for prayer, as the minister leads:

Let us all pray.

Dear God and Father of us all, we give you thanks for this man and this woman. You have brought them together by your grace. Give them now the seal of your approval, and grant them power to fulfill with pure and holy love the vow and covenant they have made. Guide them in the way of righteousness and peace, that loving and serving you with one heart and mind, they may learn also to love as you would have them love. And help us all, dear God, in each of our homes and lives, to do your will. Enrich us more and more with your grace so that, strengthening and supporting each other in the family of faith, we may serve those in need and hasten the coming of peace, love, and justice on the earth; through Jesus Christ our Lord. Amen.

† Lord's Prayer

Here the Lord's Prayer may be included:

Our Father in heaven, hallowed be your Name; your kingdom come, your will be done, on earth as in heaven. Give us today our daily bread. Forgive us our sins as we forgive those who sin against us. Save us from the time of trial and deliver us from evil. For the kingdom, the power, and the glory are yours now and forever. Amen.

† Benediction

The couple will now rise and the minister will say:

The Lord bless you and keep you; the Lord make his face to shine upon you and be gracious unto you; the Lord lift up his countenance upon you and give you peace, both now and in the life everlasting. Amen.

Here the bride and groom may kiss. Following appropriate personal greetings by the minister, the wedding party may leave the church to the accompaniment of suitable instrumental music, by the singing of a congregational hymn, or in silence.

From *The Covenant Book of Worship* (Chicago: Covenant Press, 1978), pp. 156–61. Used by permission.

5

Lutheran

† *The bride, groom, and wedding party stand in front of the minister. The parents may stand behind the couple.*

Pastor: The grace of our Lord Jesus Christ, the love of God, and the communion of the Holy Spirit be with you all.

Congregation: And also with you.

Assisting Pastor: Let us pray. Eternal God, our creator and redeemer, as you gladdened the wedding at Cana in Galilee by the presence of your Son, so by his presence now bring your joy to this wedding. Look in favor upon _____ and _____ and grant that they, rejoicing in all your gifts, may at length celebrate with Christ the marriage feast which has no end.

Congregation: Amen.

✝ *One or more lessons from the Bible may be read. An address may follow. A hymn may be sung.*

Assisting Pastor: The Lord God in his goodness created us male and female, and by the gift of marriage founded human community in a joy that begins now and is brought to perfection in the life to come.

Because of sin, our age-old rebellion, the gladness of marriage can be overcast and the gift of the family can become a burden.

But because God, who established marriage, continues still to bless it with his abundant and ever-present support, we can be sustained in our weariness and have our joy restored.

Pastor: _____ and _____, if it is your intention to share with each other your joys and sorrows and all that the years will bring, with your promises bind yourselves to each other as husband and wife.

✝ *The bride and groom face each other and join hands. Each, in turn, promises faithfulness to the other in these or similar words:*

I take you, _____,
to be my wife/husband from this day forward,
to join with you and share all that is to come,
and I promise to be faithful to you
until death parts us.

† *The bride and groom exchange rings with these words:*

I give you this ring as a sign of my love and faithfulness.

† *The bride and groom join hands, and the minister announces their marriage by saying:*

Pastor: _____ and _____, by their promises before God and in the presence of this congregation, have bound themselves to one another as husband and wife.

Congregation: Blessed be the Father and the Son and the Holy Spirit now and forever.

Pastor: Those whom God has joined together let no one put asunder.

Congregation: Amen.

† *The bride and groom kneel.*
Pastor: The Lord God, who created our first parents and established them in marriage, establish and sustain you, that you may find delight in each other and grow in holy love until your life's end.

Congregation: Amen.

† *The parents may add their blessing with these or similar words; the wedding party may join them.*

May you dwell in God's presence forever; may true and constant love preserve you.

† *The bride and groom stand.*

Assisting Pastor: Let us bless God for all the gifts in which we rejoice today.

Pastor: Lord God, constant in mercy, great in faithfulness, with high praise we recall your acts of unfailing love for the human family, for the house of Israel, and for your people the church.

We bless you for the joy which your servants, _____ and _____, have found in each other, and pray that you give to us such a sense of your constant love that we may employ all our strength in a life of praise of you, whose work alone holds true and endures forever.

Congregation: Amen.

Assisting Pastor: Let us pray for _____ and _____ in their life together.

Pastor: Faithful Lord, source of love, pour down your grace on _____ and _____, that they may fulfill the vows they have made this day and reflect your steadfast love in their life-long faithfulness to each other. As members with them of the body of Christ, use us to support their life together, and from your great store of strength give them power and patience, affection and understanding, courage, and love toward you, toward each other, and toward the world, that they may continue together in mutual growth according to your will in Jesus Christ our Lord.

Congregation: Amen.

Other intercessions may be offered.

Assisting Pastor: Let us pray for all families throughout the world.

Pastor: Gracious Father, you bless the family and renew your people. Enrich husbands and wives, parents and children more and more with your grace, that, strengthening and supporting each other, they may serve those in need and be a sign of the fulfillment of your perfect kingdom, where, with your Son Jesus Christ and the Holy Spirit, you live and reign, one God through all ages of ages.

Congregation: Amen.

✝ *When Holy Communion is celebrated, the service continues with the Peace.*
✝ *When there is no Communion, the service continues with the Lord's Prayer.*

Our Father in heaven,
hallowed be your Name,
your kingdom come,
your will be done,
on earth as in heaven.
Give us today our daily bread.
Forgive us our sins
as we forgive those
who sin against us.

Save us from the time of trial
and deliver us from evil.
For the kingdom, the power,
and the glory are yours,
now and forever. Amen.

Pastor: Almighty God, Father, Son, and Holy Spirit, keep you in his light and truth and love now and forever.

Congregation: Amen.

From *Lutheran Book of Worship* (Minneapolis: Augsburg Publishing House, 1987), pp. 202–5. Reprinted from LUTHERAN BOOK OF WORSHIP, copyright © 1987, by permission of Augsburg Fortress. May not be reproduced without permission from the publisher.

6

Methodist

The Free Methodist Church of North America

At the time set, the man and woman to be married shall stand together facing the minister, the woman on the man's left, and the minister shall say:

✝ Dearly beloved, we are gathered together here in the sight of God and the presence of these witnesses to join together this man and this woman in holy matrimony. Marriage is an honorable estate, instituted by God at the time of creation for the well-being of humankind. It is safeguarded by the laws of Moses, affirmed by the words of the prophets, and hallowed by the teachings of our Lord Jesus Christ. Marriage is a close and enduring union, a relationship in which a man and a woman forsake all others to become one flesh. This abiding union illustrates the holy relationship between Christ and his church. Marriage is therefore not to be entered into by any lightly, but reverently, soberly, and in the fear of God.

† *Addressing the man and woman, the minister shall say:*

_____ and _____, I charge you both as you stand in the presence of God to remember that covenant love alone will avail as the foundation of a happy and enduring home. Let Christ, who was loyal to his own unto death, be your example. Let the apostle Paul be your teacher, who wrote: "Love is patient and kind; love is not jealous or boastful; it is not arrogant or rude. Love does not insist on its own way; it is not irritable or resentful; it does not rejoice at wrong, but rejoices in the right. Love bears all things, believes all things, hopes all things, endures all things." If you keep this stead-fast love ever before you and, remaining faithful to each other, resolutely endeavor to fulfill the vows you now will make, God's blessing will be upon you, and the home you establish will endure through life's every change.

† *Then the minister shall say to the man, using his Christian name:*

_____, will you have _____ to be your wedded wife, to live together in the holy estate of matrimony? Will you love her, comfort her, honor and keep her, in sickness and in health; and forsaking all others, keep yourself only for her so long as you both shall live?

The man shall answer: I will.

Then the minister shall say to the woman, using her Christian name:

_____, will you have _____ to be your wedded husband, to live together in the holy estate of matrimony? Will you love him, comfort him, honor and keep him, in sickness and in health, and forsaking all others, keep yourself only for him, so long as you both shall live?

The woman shall answer: I will.

† *Then the minister shall say:*

Who gives this woman to be married to this man?

The father of the woman, or whoever gives her in marriage, shall answer: I do.

† *Then the minister, receiving the hand of the woman from her father or other sponsor, shall ask the man with his right hand to take the woman by her right hand, and say after him:*

I, _____, take you, _____, to be my wedded wife, to have and to hold, from this day forward, in plenty and in want, in joy and in sorrow, in sickness and in health, to love and to cherish till death us do part, and thereto I pledge you my faith.

Then they shall loose their hands, and the woman, with her right hand, shall take the man by his right hand, and shall likewise say after the minister:

I, _____, take you, _____, to be my wedded husband, to have and to hold, from this day forward, in plenty and in want, in joy and in sorrow, in sickness and in health, to love and to cherish till death us do part, and thereto I pledge you my faith.

† *Then they shall again loose hands. The grooms-man may give to the minister a ring, which the minister in turn will give to the groom, who will put it on the third finger of the woman's left hand and, holding the ring, shall say after the minister:*

This ring I give you in token and pledge of our constant faith and steadfast love.

In case of a double ring ceremony, the minister shall receive the other ring from the bridesmaid and shall give it to the woman to put on the third finger of the man's left hand. The woman, holding the ring there, shall say after the minister:

This ring I give you in token and pledge of our constant faith and steadfast love.

Then the minister shall say: Let us pray.

† O Eternal God, creator and preserver of all humankind, giver of all spiritual grace, the author of everlasting life, send your blessing on this man and this woman whom we bless in your Name; that they, living faithfully together, may surely perform and keep the vow and covenant made between them, and may ever remain in perfect love and peace together, and live according to your laws through Jesus Christ our Lord. Amen.

† *Then the minister shall say:*

Forasmuch as _____ and _____ have consented together in holy wedlock and have witnessed the same before God and this company and have pledged their faith to each other and have declared the same by joining hands (and by giving and receiving a ring), therefore, by the authority granted to me as a minister of Jesus Christ, I pronounce that they are husband and wife together, in the Name of the Father, and of the Son, and of the Holy Spirit. Those whom God has joined together, let not man put asunder. Amen.

† *The man and woman then kneel, and the minister shall pray over them an extemporaneous prayer, prepared especially for the two of them.*

† *The man and woman shall stand, and the minister shall pronounce over them the following benediction:*

Go forth into the world in peace.
Be of good courage.
Hold fast to that which is good.
Render to no one evil for evil.
Strengthen the faint hearted,
Support the weak,
Help the afflicted,
Show honor to all.
Love and serve the Lord,
Rejoicing in the power of the Holy Spirit.
And the blessing of God Almighty,
The Father,
The Son,
And the Holy Spirit,
Be upon you and remain with you forever.
Amen.

From the *Book of Discipline 1989, Part A* (Indianapolis: Free Methodist Publishing House, 1989), pp. 191–94. Used by permission.

The Wesleyan Church

At the day and time appointed for the solemnizing of matrimony, the persons to be married standing together, the man on the right hand of the woman, the minister shall say:

✝ Dearly beloved, we are gathered together in the sight of God, and in the presence of these witnesses, to join together this man and this woman in holy matrimony, which is an honorable estate, instituted of God, and signifying unto us the mystical union that exists between Christ and his church. This holy estate Christ adorned and beautified with his presence in Cana of Galilee, and the apostle Paul commended as honorable among all men. It is not therefore to be entered into unadvisedly, but reverently, discreetly, and in the fear of God.

✝ *Speaking to the persons to be married, the minister shall say:*

I require and charge you both, as you stand in the presence of God, to remember that love and loyalty alone will avail as the foundation of a happy and enduring home. No other human ties are more tender, no other vow more sacred than those you now assume. If these solemn vows be faithfully kept, and if steadfastly you endeavor to do the will of your heavenly Father, your life will be full of joy, and the home you are establishing will abide in peace.

† *Then the minister shall address the man by name, and ask:*

Will you have this woman to be your wedded wife, to live together after God's ordinance in the holy estate of matrimony? Will you love her, comfort her, honor and keep her, in sickness and in health; and forsaking all others keep yourself only unto her, so long as you both shall live?

The man shall answer: I will.

Then the minister shall address the woman by name, and ask:

Will you have this man to be your wedded husband, to live together after God's ordinance in the holy estate of matrimony? Will you love him, comfort him, honor and keep him, in sickness and in health; and forsaking all others, keep yourself only unto him, so long as you both shall live?

The woman shall answer: I will.

✝ *Then the minister shall ask:*
Who gives this woman to be married to this man?

The father of the woman, or whoever gives her in marriage, shall answer:

I do (*or* Her mother and I).

✝ *Then the minister shall ask the man and woman to join right hands and shall ask the man, using their given names, to say after him:*

I, _____, take you, _____, to be my wedded wife, to have and to hold, from this day forward, for better, for worse, for richer, for poorer, in sickness and in health, to love and to cherish, till death do us part, according to God's holy law; and thereto I pledge you my faith.

Then the minister shall ask the woman, using their given names, to say after him:

I, _____, take you, _____, to be my wedded husband, to have and to hold, from this day forward, for better, for worse, for richer, for poorer, in sickness and in health, to love and to cherish, till death do us part, according to God's holy law; and thereto I pledge you my faith.

✝ *Then the minister shall say:*
By seeking the ministry of the church, you have expressed your conviction that marriage is more than a legal contract, but rather a bond of union sealed in heaven. Henceforth, you shall no longer be two but one. Your paths will be united; your re-

sponsibilities will increase, but your strength and your joys will be multiplied if you are sincere and earnest in your relations one to the other, and with God who has witnessed and sealed this covenant. Let us pray.

Here may be offered the following prayer, or an extemporaneous prayer closing with the Lord's Prayer.

O eternal God, creator and preserver of all humankind, giver of all spiritual grace, the author of life everlasting, let your blessing descend and rest on these your children, whom we bless in your Name. Bless this marriage and make it to them the source of abundant and enduring good. Look graciously on them that they may love, honor, and cherish each other. May their mutual affection never know change, doubt, or decay. Direct and strengthen them in the discharge of all their duties. Bless the home that they establish. Teach them to order their household wisely and well, and to regard all their possessions as your gifts to be employed in your service. May they so live together in faithfulness and patience, in wisdom and true godliness, that their home may be a haven of blessing and a place of peace, through Jesus Christ our Lord. Amen.

✝ *Then the minister shall ask the man and woman to join right hands and placing his hand on top of theirs shall say:*

Forasmuch as _____ and _____ have consented together in holy wedlock, and have witnessed the same before God, and this company, and thereto have pledged their faith each to the other, and have declared the same by joining hands; I pronounce that they are husband and wife together, in the Name of the Father, and of the Son, and of the Holy Spirit. Those whom God hath joined together let not man put asunder. Amen.

† God the Father, God the Son, God the Holy Spirit, bless, preserve, and keep you; the Lord mercifully with his favor look upon you, and so fill you with all spiritual benediction and grace, that you may so live together in this life, that in the world to come you may have life everlasting. Amen.

From *The Discipline* (Indianapolis: Wesley Press, 1989), pp. 407–9. Used by permission.

7

Presbyterian

Presbyterian Church in America

✝ *At the time and place appointed for the solemnization of matrimony, the persons to be married shall take their places before the minister, the man having the woman at his left hand, and all present reverently standing. The minister shall say:*

Dearly beloved, we are gathered here in the presence of God to join this man and this woman in holy matrimony.

Marriage was instituted by God himself in the time of man's innocence and uprightness. The Lord God said, "It is not good that the man should be alone; I will make him a helper comparable to him" (Gen. 2:18). Thereupon God created woman of man's own substance and brought her to the man. Our Lord Jesus Christ honored marriage by his presence at the wedding in Cana of Galilee. And he confirmed it as a divine ordinance and a union not to be severed when he declared, "Therefore what God hath joined together, let not man separate" (Matt. 19:6). Moreover, the apostle Paul set forth the sacred and exalted nature of marriage when he likened it to the mystical union that subsists between Christ and his church.

The purpose of marriage is the enrichment of the lives of those who enter into this estate, the propagation of the race, and the extension of Christ's church to the glory of the covenant God.

† Let us reverently hear what the Holy Scriptures teach concerning the duty of husbands to their wives and of wives to their husbands:

"Husbands, love your wives, just as Christ also loved the church, and gave himself up for it; that he might sanctify, and cleanse it with the washing of water by the Word. . . . So husbands ought to love their own wives as their own bodies" (Eph. 5:25–28).

"Wives, submit to your own husbands, as to the Lord. For the husband is the head of the wife, as also Christ is the head of the church, and he is the Savior of the body" (Eph. 5:22–23).

These two persons are come to be joined in this holy estate of marriage. If any man can show just cause why they may not lawfully be wedded, let him now declare it, or else hereafter forever hold his peace.

I require and charge you both that, if either of you knows any cause why you may not be lawfully joined together in matrimony, you do now confess it.

✝ Let us pray:

Most holy and most merciful Father, at once the God of nature and of grace, creator, preserver, and redeemer of humankind, fill these, your servant and your handmaiden, with a sense of the solemnity of the vows they are about to make. May they look to you for your assistance, and enter into these sacred obligations in humble dependence on your enabling grace. Grant this, O Father, with the forgiveness of our sins, through Jesus Christ, your Son. Amen.

✝ *After prayer the minister shall say:*

Who giveth this woman to be married to this man?

The father of the woman, or someone in his stead, shall place her right hand in that of the minister, and the minister shall ask the man to take with his right hand the right hand of the woman. The minister shall then say:

_____, will you have this woman to be your wedded wife, to live with her after God's commandments in the holy estate of marriage? And will you love her, honor and cherish her, so long as you both shall live?

The man shall answer: I will.

Then the minister shall say:

_____, will you have this man to be your wedded husband, to live with him after God's commandments in the holy estate of marriage? And will you love him, cherish and obey him, so long as you both shall live?

The woman shall answer: I will.

✝ *The man shall say:*

I, _____, take you, _____, to be my wedded wife, and I do promise and covenant before God and these witnesses to be your loving and faithful husband in sickness and in health, in plenty and in want, in joy and in sorrow, as long as we both shall live.

The woman shall say:

I, _____, take you, _____, to be my wedded husband, and I do promise and covenant before God and these witnesses to be your loving and faithful wife in sickness and in health, in plenty and in want, in joy and in sorrow, as long as we both shall live.

✝ *The man shall then put the ring on the third finger of the woman's left hand, and shall say after the minister:*

This ring I give you as a symbol and pledge of constant faith and abiding love.

The minister shall say to the woman:

Do you, _____, receive this ring as a token of your pledge to keep this covenant and perform these vows?

The woman shall say: I do.

✝ *The minister shall say:*
Let us pray.

✝ *After prayer the minister shall say:*

By virtue of the authority committed unto me by the church of Christ and the law of the state, I now pronounce you, _____, and _____, husband and wife, in the Name of the Father and of the Son and of the Holy Spirit. Amen.

✝ *The minister shall ask the husband and wife to join their right hands, and shall say:*

"What God hath joined together, let no man put asunder." The Lord our God fill you with his grace, and grant that you may long live together in all godliness and holiness. Amen.

This form was derived from the PCUS Book of Church Order as approved in 1893, and from the OPC Book as approved in 1940. *The Book of Church Order of the Presbyterian Church in America* (Decatur, Ga.: Committee for Christian Education and Publications, 1983). Used by permission.

8

Reformed

Christian Reformed Church

† Declaration of Purpose

We have come together before the face of God to join _____ and _____ in marriage. We seek to honor the will of God for marriage, the concern of the Christian church for its well-being, and the interest of the state in the orderly development of society.

† Invocation

God, our Father, we praise you for making and redeeming us to live together in love. We thank you for the love and trust that bring _____ and _____ to this their marriage day. Favor them with the honor of your presence at their wedding. Unite them by your Spirit so that together they may reflect the love of Christ for his church. Through Jesus Christ our Lord. Amen.

† Parting from Parents (optional)

Today _____ and _____ leave their parents to establish a new home.

Do you, Mr. and Mrs. [*parents of the groom*], give your blessing to them and promise them your continued love and support?

They answer: We give them our blessing, and so promise, God helping us.

Do you, Mr. and Mrs. [*parents of the bride*], give your blessing to them and promise them your continued love and support?

They answer: We give them our blessing, and so promise, God helping us.

† Institution and Meaning of Marriage

In marriage, as instituted by God, a man and a woman covenant to live together in a lifelong, exclusive partnership of love and fidelity (Gen. 2:18; Matt. 19:5–6). The apostle Paul sees the union of husband and wife as a symbol of the union between Christ and his church (Eph. 5:31–32). If marriage is to be pleasing in the sight of God, those who enter into this covenant of life must share a common commitment to the Lord of life.

In putting his blessing on a marriage, God intended that it would provide:

- a context within which husband and wife can help and comfort each other and find companionship;

- a setting within which we may give loving and tender expression to the desires God gave us;

- a secure environment within which children may be born and taught to know and serve the Lord; and

- a structure that enriches society and contributes to its orderly function.

When these purposes are prayerfully pursued in union with Christ, the kingdom of God is advanced and the blessedness of husband and wife assured.

In Ephesians 5 the apostle Paul admonishes all Christians to develop a mutual respect and love when he says, "Submit to one another out of reverence for Christ." When he applies this to the marriage relationship, he instructs the wife to be subject to her husband as the church is subject to

Christ, its head. He also instructs the husband to pattern his love for his wife after the example of Christ's love for his body, the church. Paul says, "Wives, submit to your husbands as to the Lord," and "Husbands, love your wives, just as Christ loved the church and gave himself up for her." In marriage this requires that the husband and wife serve each other by providing the love, nurture, and faith that will enrich their lives together and build a Christ-centered home.

Our sinful and selfish tendency to break down what God has built threatens marriage with tensions, agony, and even with broken bonds. People who marry in the Lord, however, may trust that he will lead them and graciously provide for their needs when they follow the biblical pattern for love. "Love is patient, love is kind. It does not envy, it does not boast, it is not proud. It is not rude, it is not self-seeking, it is not easily angered, it keeps no record of wrongs. Love does not delight in evil but rejoices with the truth. It always protects, always trusts, always hopes, always perseveres. Love never fails" (1 Cor. 13:4–8a).

† Declaration of Intent

_____ and _____, now that you have heard God's message concerning marriage, do you agree with it and do you commit yourselves to each other in accordance with it?

Each answers: I do.

† Exchange of Vows

In the presence of God and before these people I now invite you to exchange your vows.

Groom: I take you, _____, to be my wife and I promise before God and all who are present here to be your loving and faithful husband, as long as our lives shall last. I will love you and give myself up for you, as Christ loved the church and gave himself up for her. I will serve you with tenderness and respect, and encourage you to develop the gifts that God has given you.

Bride: I take you, _____, to be my husband, and I promise before God and all who are present here to be your loving and faithful wife, as long as our lives shall last. I will love you and submit to you, as the church loves and submits to Christ. I will serve you with tenderness and respect, and encourage you to develop the gifts that God has given you.

† Exchange of Rings (optional)

Groom: _____, I give you this ring as a symbol of our covenant in Christ.

Bride: _____, I give you this ring as a symbol of our covenant in Christ.

† Declaration of Marriage

As a minister of the church of Christ and by the authority which the state has vested in me, I now pronounce you, _____ and _____, husband and wife, in the Name of the Father, Son, and Holy Spirit. Amen. "Therefore what God has joined together, let man not separate" (Matt. 19:6).

† Promise of Support (optional)

Do you who are present here promise to pray for _____ and _____ and support them as times and circumstances may require?

People: We do, God helping us.

† Pastor's Message

† Prayer Following a Marriage Ceremony

Father in heaven,
give today your blessing
upon the marriage of _____
and _____.
We thank you for the vows
they have spoken
and the love in which
they are now united.
Keep them faithful and strong
in every trial.

71

Sustain their joy and affection
for many years.
We pray, Lord Jesus,
that you will be acknowledged
head of their home
and master of their lives.
Equip them, Holy Spirit,
with patient endurance,
sacrificial service, unfailing
courtesy,
endless trust, and lasting love.
Grant that their home
will often be a place of laughter;
and in times of difficulty or trouble,
a haven of healing and forgiveness.
May they and their children
give constant praise to you,
eternal Father, who with the Son
and the Spirit
is God, blessed and exalted forever.
Amen.

This form, adopted by the Christian Reformed Church Synod of 1979, includes an optional concluding prayer adopted in 1981. The vows were revised by the Synod of 1986. From the *Psalter Hymnal* (Grand Rapids: CRC Publications, 1987), pp. 1010–12. Used by permission.

Reformed Church in America

The Approach to God

The service of worship may begin with instrumental and/or choral music in praise of God. When the wedding party has assembled they may approach the front of the church during the following:

† Processional Hymn

All present shall stand to sing, and remain standing through the salutation.

† Votum

Our help is in the Name of the Lord who made heaven and earth. Amen.

† Sentences

One of the following or another appropriate scriptural sentence shall be read.

I will sing of the Lord's great love forever; with my mouth I will make your faithfulness known to all generations. I will declare that your love stands firm forever, that you established your faithfulness in heaven itself (Ps. 89:1–2).

Or:

O servants of the Lord, you that stand in the house of the Lord, in the courts of the house of our God! Praise the Lord, for the Lord is good; sing to his name, for he is gracious! (Ps. 135:1b–3).

† Salutation

Grace and peace be yours in fullest measure, through the knowledge of God and Jesus our Lord. Amen. (2 Peter 1:2).

† Declaration of Purpose

After the people have been seated, the minister shall say:

We are gathered here to praise God for the covenant of grace and reconciliation made with us through Jesus Christ, to hear it proclaimed anew, and to respond to it as we witness the covenant of marriage _____ and _____ make with each other in Christ's Name.

Christian marriage is a joyful covenanting between a man and a woman in which they proclaim, before God and human witnesses, their commitment to live together in spiritual, physical, and material unity. In this covenant they acknowledge that the great love God has shown for each of them enables them to love each other. They affirm that God's gracious presence and abiding power are needed for them to keep their vows, to continue to live in love, and to be faithful servants of Christ in this world. For human commitment is fragile and human love imperfect, but the promise of God is eternal and the love of God can bring our love to perfection.

The Word of God

† Prayer

Let us pray.

Most gracious God, be with us in this time of joy and celebration. Reveal the good news of your love for us in the proclamation of your Word. Enable us to respond to you with faithfulness and obedience, so that in all we do and say your Name may be praised. Through Jesus Christ our Lord we pray. Amen.

† Lessons

One or more lessons from Scripture shall be read. If there is only one lesson, it shall be from the New Testament.

† Sermon

The minister may preach a brief sermon relating the Word of God to the response of Christian marriage.

† Prayer for Blessing

Almighty God, through your grace write these words in our hearts, that they may bring forth in us the fruits of the Spirit, to the honor and praise of your Name, through Jesus Christ our Lord. Amen.

The Response to God

† Declaration of Consent

The persons to be married shall stand with their attendants before the minister, who shall ask the man:

_____ , will you receive _____ as your wife and bind yourself to her in the covenant of marriage? Will you promise to love and honor her in true devotion; to rejoice with her in times of felicity and grieve with her in times of sorrow; and be faithful to her as long as you both shall live?

I will, with the help of God.

The minister shall ask the woman:

_____, will you receive _____ as your husband and bind yourself to him in the covenant of marriage? Will you promise to love and honor him in true devotion; to rejoice with him in times of felicity and grieve with him in times of sorrow; and be faithful to him as long as you both shall live?

I will, with the help of God.

The minister shall ask the family members of the persons to be married to stand. When they have done so, the minister shall ask:

Will you receive _____ and _____ into your family and uphold them with your love as they establish themselves a family within your own?

We will.

The minister shall ask all present to stand. When they have done so, the minister shall ask:

Will you who witness this covenant between _____ and _____ respect their marriage and sustain them with your friendship and care?

We will.

† Vows

The minister shall say to the man and the woman:

_____ and _____, before God and these witnesses, make your covenant of marriage with each other.

Vows may be exchanged according to Form 1 or Form 2 below:

Form 1

The man shall face the woman, take her hand in his, and say:

I, _____, take you, _____, to be my wife,
to have and to hold from this day forward,
for better, for worse,
for richer, for poorer,
in sickness and in health,
to love and to cherish
as long as we both shall live.
To this I pledge myself
truly with all my heart.

The minister shall receive the ring from its bearer and give it to the man, who shall place it on the hand of the woman and say:

This ring I give in token of the covenant made this day between us, in the Name of the Father and of the Son and of the Holy Spirit.

The woman, still facing the man and taking his hand in hers, shall say:

I, _____, take you, _____, to be my husband,
to have and to hold from this day forward,
for better, for worse,
for richer, for poorer,

in sickness and in health,
to love and to cherish
as long as we both shall live.
To this I pledge myself
truly with all my heart.

The minister shall receive the ring from its bearer and give it to the woman, who shall place it on the hand of the man and say:

This ring I give in token of the covenant made this day between us, in the Name of the Father and of the Son and of the Holy Spirit.

Form 2

The man and the woman shall face each other and take hands. They shall say to each other, in turn:

_____,
I give myself to you in marriage
and vow to be your husband (wife)
all the days of our lives.
I give you my hands
and take your hands in mine
as a symbol and pledge
of our uniting in one flesh.
I give you my love,
the outpouring of my heart,
as a symbol and pledge
of our uniting in one spirit.

I give you this ring
from out of my worldly goods
as a symbol and pledge
of our uniting as one family.

After each has said the vows, he/she shall take the ring from the minister and place it on the other's hand.

† Blessing

Prayer may be offered according to Form 1 or Form 2. The minister may ask the married persons to kneel, or to remain standing and face the minister.

Form 1

Let us ask for the blessing of the Lord.
Eternal God,
in whom we live and move and have our being,
bless _____ and _____
that they may live together in marriage
according to the vows they have made before you.
Bless them with your love,
that their love for each other
may grow ever deeper,
and their love for you may shine forth
before the world.
Bless them with your mercy,
that they may be patient and caring,

willing to share each other's joys and sorrows,
to forgive and to be forgiven,
in their life together and in the world.
Bless them with your peace,
that they may be calm and sure,
trusting in you with confident hearts
and living in harmony and concord
within their family and among all people.
Bless them with your presence,
that within their hearts and their home
Christ may reign as head,
and that they may acknowledge his Lordship
with praise and thanksgiving
now, and through all their life together,
to the glory of your holy Name! Amen.

Form 2

Let us pray.

O God, Creator of life, Author of Salvation, and Giver of all good gifts, look with favor upon _____ and _____ who have covenanted marriage in your Name. Bless their union, and sustain them in their devotion to each other and to you.

Grant them the desire to order their lives according to your will, that in their relationship with each other, and those around them, they may show forth the joy and peace of Christ.

Sustain them in the seasons and conditions of their lives by the power of your Holy Spirit, that in joy and sorrow, leisure and labor, plenty and want, they may give thanks for your steadfast love and declare your faithfulness before the world.

Increase in them the will to grow in faith and service to Christ. Let their life together bear witness to the healing and reconciling love of Christ for this troubled, broken world.

Give them a deep appreciation of the unity of all persons within your creation, that their love for each other may be reflected also in their desire for justice, dignity, and meaning for all your children.

Keep ever vivid in their hearts a vision of your kingdom, and enable them to live in the hope of its fulfillment. By the power of your Spirit, O God, accomplish these petitions as they accord with your will, for we pray through Jesus Christ our Lord. Amen.

† Declaration

_____ and _____ have made their covenant of marriage together before God and all here present, by solemn vows, by the joining of hands, and by the giving and receiving of rings. Therefore, I declare that they are husband and wife; in the Name of the Father and of the Son and of the Holy Spirit.

And (to the couple):

Be united; live in peace, and the God of peace and love will be with you (2 Cor. 13:11).

Or (to all present):

They are no longer two, therefore, but one body. So then, what God has united, no one may divide (Matt. 19:6). Amen.

† Peace

The husband and wife greet each other with the kiss of peace.

† Benediction

The grace of the Lord Jesus Christ, the love of God, and the fellowship of the Holy Spirit be with you all (2 Cor. 13:14). Amen.

† Recessional Hymn

A hymn of thanksgiving may be sung, or instrumental music played, during which the married persons and their attendants may recess.

From James R. Esther and Donald J. Bruggink, *Worship the Lord* (Grand Rapids: Eerdmans, 1987), pp. 30–35. Used by permission.

PART 2

Alternate Wedding Ceremonies

9

Contemporary Weddings

Option One

✛ **Prelude**

✛ **Special Music**

✛ **Lighting of Candles**

Ushers or the mothers of bride and groom light outer candles of unity candelabra.

✛ **Processional**

✠ Words of Welcome

We warmly welcome each of you to this joyful occasion of the marriage of _____ and _____. The Lord God has said, "It is not good for the man to be alone. I will make a helper suitable for him. . . . Then the Lord God made a woman from the rib he had taken out of the man, and he brought her to the man. The man said, 'This is now bone of my bones and flesh of my flesh.' . . . For this reason a man will leave his father and mother and be united to his wife, and they will become one flesh" (Gen. 2:18, 22–24). Because God intended marriage to bring blessing and joy, let us invoke his presence prior to entering this holy covenant.

✠ Invocation

Lord God, our Father, Creator, and Redeemer, we come desiring to acknowledge you in all of our ways, in order that you might direct our steps. Especially do we need you to be present and direct our steps on such a special occasion as this. We pray that you might graciously pour out your richest blessings on this couple who stand before us in your presence to assume the privileges and responsibilities of Christian marriage. May you guide them step by step from this day forth as they begin their journey together as husband and wife. Throughout this wedding ceremony may the beauty of Jesus Christ be with us. We humbly ask this in his exalted Name. Amen.

✠ Scripture Reading

✠ Parting from Parents

Today _____ and _____ leave their parents to establish a new home as husband and wife. I would ask the parents of _____ and _____ to add their blessing to this marriage.

Parents of groom: We, the parents of _____, thank God that in his providence he has brought these two people together to be married. We welcome _____ into our family, and trust that God will richly bless this home that he is establishing.

Parents of bride: We, the parents of _____, thank God that in his providence he has brought these two people together to be married. We welcome _____ into our family, and trust that God will richly bless this home that he is establishing.

✠ Declaration of Intent

Minister to the groom: Before God and these witnesses, will you, _____, take _____ to be your wife? Will you love and comfort her, honor and keep her, and in joy and sorrow, preserve with her

89

this bond, holy and unbroken, until the return of Christ Jesus, or as long as you both shall live?

Groom: I will.

   Minister to the bride: Before God and these witnesses, will you, _____, take _____ to be your husband? Will you love and comfort him, honor and keep him, and in joy and sorrow, preserve with him this bond, holy and unbroken, until the return of Christ Jesus, or as long as you both shall live?

Bride: I will.

✠ Congregational Hymn or Musical Selection

✠ Exchange of Vows

   The bride and groom shall turn and face each other, joining hands.

Groom: I, _____, take you, _____, to be my wife, to love you with all my heart, to share my life with you, and to be faithful to you in an exclusive Christian marriage.

Bride: I, _____, take you, _____, to be my husband, to love you with all my heart, to share my life with you,

90

and to be faithful to you in an exclusive Christian marriage.

✚ Exchange of Rings

May we now have the rings?

These rings have no beginning and no end. They set forth the eternal nature of real love. They will represent the love and trust that _____ and _____ promise to each other this day.

To groom: _____, will you take this ring and place it upon _____'s finger, and as you do, repeat to her, after me, these words:

I give you this ring as a token of my love and commitment to live with you in a Christian marriage from this day forward. In the Name of the Father, Son, and Holy Spirit. Amen.

To bride: _____, will you take this ring and place it upon _____'s finger, and as you do, repeat to him, after me, these words:

I give you this ring as a token of my love and commitment to live with you in a Christian marriage from this day forward. In the Name of the Father, Son, and Holy Spirit. Amen.

✠ Prayer of Dedication

The couple may kneel for this prayer, which may then be followed by a musical selection.

✠ Lighting of Unity Candle

✠ Pronouncement of Marriage

Inasmuch as _____ and _____ have exchanged vows and rings, before God and the gathered witnesses, by virtue of the authority entrusted to me as a minister of Christ's church, and in agreement with the laws of the state, I now pronounce them husband and wife. "What God has joined together, let man not separate."

At this point the bride and groom may embrace and kiss.

✠ Option: Communion Service

✠ Benediction

The Lord bless you
and keep you;
the Lord make his face shine upon you
and be gracious to you;
the Lord turn his face toward you
and give you peace.

In the Name of the Father, Son, and Holy Spirit. Amen.

✠ Introduction of Newlyweds

I count it an honor to be the first to introduce to you Mr. and Mrs. _____.

✠ Recessional

As bride and groom recess they stop to give a rose to each other's mothers.

Option Two

✠ **Prelude and Lighting of Candles**

✠ **Processional**

✠ **Call to Worship**—Psalm 95:1–7

✠ **Hymn or Song of Praise**

✠ **Responsive Sentences**

Minister: This is the message that you have heard from the beginning: that we should love one another.

People: Let us love one another, for love is from God and is of the nature of life, and the one who has loved has known God.

Minister: In the beginning God said, "It is not good for the man to be alone. I will make a helper suitable for him."

People: A man will leave his father and mother and be united to his wife, and they will become one flesh.

Minister: Praise be to God for the gift of Christian marriage.

✚ Musical Selection

✚ Words of Greeting

We warmly welcome each of you who come to participate in this joyful and happy occasion in the life of _____ and _____. You have been asked to share as witnesses to the covenant they make to each other in the presence of God. Let us together acknowledge the Lord's presence as we pray together as Christ taught us to pray . . .

✚ The Lord's Prayer

✚ Questions to Bride and Groom

Are both of you ready to enter into this covenant of marriage, to accept the responsibilities of being husband and wife, whatever circumstances the future may hold? If so, please join hands and answer, "I am ready, with the help of the Lord."

✝ Questions to Parents

God's intention was that we leave our parents to be joined to our husband or wife. When a father agrees to "give his daughter away," he is endorsing this biblical principle, and giving his consent to his daughter's marriage. He is willingly forfeiting the primary place that he and his wife have had in the life of their daughter. He is giving his blessing to the marriage.

With that understanding, let me ask: Who gives this woman to be married to this man?

Father and mother of bride: We do.

Do the parents of the groom, likewise, give your son to be married to this woman?

Father and mother of groom: We do.

Pastor to both sets of parents: Do you give your blessing to _____ and _____ in this new relationship of marriage? Do you support them with your love and agree to give them the freedom to grow together as a new, separate family unit under the Lordship of Christ?

Parents: We do.

✝ Musical Selection

✠ Wedding Vows

Bride and groom turn and face each other, joining hands.

Groom: I, _____, having full confidence in the grace of Christ, take you, _____, to be my wedded wife. I promise to be your loving and faithful husband, in prosperity and in need, in joy and in sorrow, in sickness and in health, as long as we both shall live.

Bride: I, _____, having full confidence in the grace of Christ, take you, _____, to be my wedded husband. I promise to be your loving and faithful wife, in prosperity and in need, in joy and in sorrow, in sickness and in health, as long as we both shall live.

✠ Exchange of Rings

Let us pray. Our Father in heaven, bless this man and woman, that having promised to live together as husband and wife, you will strengthen and enable them to keep these vows. We pray for your blessing on them and on their home from this day forward. May your presence be evident in their home and in every area of their relationship together. May the rings they now place on each other's fingers serve as a continual reminder of the vows made this day. We pray this in the Name of Christ Jesus our Lord. Amen.

Groom: I give you this ring as a token of our marriage covenant, in the Name of the Father, Son, and Holy Spirit. Amen.

Bride: I give you this ring as a token of our marriage covenant, in the Name of the Father, Son, and Holy Spirit. Amen.

✢ Brief Wedding Meditation

✢ Prayer of Dedication

By minister or selected members of the wedding party or relatives.

✢ Declaration of Marriage

_____ and _____, since you have promised your love to each other in the presence of God and these witnesses, and have exchanged vows and rings, I pronounce that you are husband and wife. What God has joined together, let no one separate. In the Name of the Father, Son, and Holy Spirit. Amen.

✢ Lighting of Unity Candle

✢ Hymn or Musical Selection

✠ Benediction

May the grace of the Lord Jesus Christ, and the love of God the Father, and the fellowship of the Holy Spirit, be with you all. Amen.

✠ Embrace

You may now kiss your bride.

✠ Recessional

10

Service of Recognition
of a Civil Marriage

✠ *Minister:* Brothers and sisters in Christ, _____
and _____ have been married by the law of the
state, and they have taken vows to be husband and
wife. Now, in faith, they come before the church to
acknowledge their marriage covenant and to bear
witness to their common purpose in Christ.

✠ Marriage is God's loving gift to humans. In
marriage a man and a woman bind themselves in
love and become one in the Lord, even as Christ is
one with the church, his body. Christ has declared
that a man shall leave his father and mother and
cleave to his wife. The Lord has established marriage from the beginning for our welfare and hap-

piness. _____ and _____, be subject to one another out of reverence for Christ.

✠ *Minister to the man:* Please repeat after me these words of promise to your wife:

_____, you are my wife. With the Lord's grace I promise to be your faithful husband, forsaking all others, to love and serve you as Christ commands, in sickness and in health, in joy and in sorrow, for as long as we both shall live.

Minister to the woman: Please repeat after me these words of promise to your husband:

_____, you are my husband. With the Lord's grace I promise to be your faithful wife, forsaking all others, to love and serve you as Christ commands, in sickness and in health, in joy and in sorrow, for as long as we both shall live.

✠ *A ring(s) may be given, with the givers repeating the following words:*

In the Name of the Father, Son, and Holy Spirit, I give you this ring as a sign of my marriage commitment.

✠ *The minister addresses the congregation saying,*
Will you who have witnessed these promises do all in your ability, by God's grace, to uphold and encourage these two persons in their marriage? If so, answer "We will."

People: We will.

✠ Let us pray. Eternal Father, Creator of marriage, we acknowledge that without your grace no promise is sure. Strengthen _____ and _____ with the gift of your Spirit, so that they might fulfill the vows they have taken in your presence. Keep them faithful to you and to each other. Fill them with such love and joy that they may build a home where Christ is honored. And guide them by your word to serve you all the days of their lives; through Jesus Christ our Lord, to whom be honor and glory, both now and forever. Amen.

✠ *After the man and woman have joined hands, the minister shall say:*

_____ and _____, you are husband and wife according to the witness of the holy Christian church. Help each other. Be united; live in peace, and the God of love and peace will be with you. What God has joined together, may no one separate.

✠ Receive now the benediction: May the Lord bless, preserve, and keep you. The grace of the Lord Jesus Christ and the love of God the Father and the fellowship of the Holy Spirit be with you today and throughout your life together. Amen.

11

A Brief Wedding Ceremony

✠ Words of Greeting

When Jesus was called to the wedding at Cana in Galilee, he gladly joined the happy celebration and began his ministry with acts of power. Ever since that day the entrance of Christ into homes that welcome him has been occasion for rich blessing. His presence brings spiritual strength and increasing joy. Today _____ and _____ desire the companionship of Christ at the outset of their wedded life. They have invited us to be witnesses before the Lord of the promises they are about to make.

✠ Words to the Bride and Groom

This Christian wedding ceremony is rooted in God's creation of marriage from the very beginning. He designed marriage in his wisdom to enable us to handle the difficulties of life as well as to be a source of companionship and joy. May this be true for you as you purpose in your hearts to honor Christ, and to exercise patience and sacrifice for the good of one another. As you come to the threshold of a new life together, I encourage you to take your vows with earnest dependence on the grace of Christ.

✠ Declaration of Intent

To the groom: _____, do you before God and these witnesses take this woman to be your lawfully wedded wife; and do you promise that from this day forward you will be her faithful husband, for better or worse, for richer or poorer, in sickness and in health, to love and to cherish, till death do you part?

Groom: I do.

To the bride: _____, do you before God and these witnesses take this man to be your lawfully wedded husband; and do you promise that from this day forward you will be his faithful wife, for better or worse, for richer or poorer, in sickness and in health, to love and to cherish till death do you part?

Bride: I do.

✚ Exchange of Rings and Vows

The ring is given to the groom, who places it on the bride's finger, and repeats after the minister:

I, _____, take you, _____, to be my wedded wife. And I promise and covenant, before God and these witnesses, to be your loving and faithful husband; in plenty and in want, in joy and in sorrow, in sickness and in health, for as long as we both shall live.

The other ring is given to the bride, who places it on the groom's finger, and repeats after the minister:

I, _____, take you, _____, to be my wedded husband. And I promise and covenant, before God and these witnesses, to be your loving and faithful wife; in plenty and in want, in joy and in sorrow, in sickness and in health, as long as we both shall live.

✚ Prayer

(May be followed by the Lord's Prayer)

105

✠ Pronouncement

_____ and _____ have promised to take each other as husband and wife to live together in a Christian marriage. They have given rings as a token of this covenant. Therefore they now enter into the holy state of matrimony. As a minister of the Gospel of Jesus Christ, I now pronounce them husband and wife. What God has joined together, let no one separate.

✠ Benediction

The Lord bless you
and keep you.
The Lord make his face to shine upon you
and be gracious to you;
the Lord turn his face toward you
and give you peace.
In the Name of the Father, Son, and Holy Spirit.
Amen.

12

Ceremony for a Remarriage of a Couple with Children

✠ The Prologue

My friends, we are gathered here for the purpose both solemn and beautiful, both spiritual and of the earth. We are going to witness the marriage of _____ and _____, who have already promised themselves to each other in their hearts. It is a moment of enormous significance in their lives—perhaps of more significance than anything they have done in a long, long time or will ever do again; for from this moment their lives will grow differently—they will grow together. The way they see the world will be different. The way they relate to others will be different. And the way they know and experience each other will be different.

They are not beginners in life. Each has had a certain lifetime already, with experiences of pleasure and pain, of joy and agony, of discovery and growth. But their times for such experiences are not over. Their union, celebrated here today and forged by the days and years that lie ahead, will lead to new pleasures and pains, new times of discovery and growth. Therefore, this is a mystical time in their journeys, a time of great spiritual possibility. And thus it is a time to be remembered and celebrated before the altar of God, where the burning of candles symbolizes the presence of the Holy.

Because it is a time of spirit and celebration, we will pause to pray:

O God, who blesses all lives that are yielded to you in faith and sincerity, and without whom no life is ever blessed, we bow in your presence at the outset of this sacred experience. Give us all a sense of reverence for what we are about to do. Throughout human history, you have been especially close to persons whose lives were being brought into new relationships through marriage. Now, as _____ and _____ are joined before this altar, let us feel your closeness to them. Hallow the words we use and the air we breathe. Let the spirit and solemnity of this time never be lost to our memories, through him who loves us and sanctifies all our deeds, even Christ our Lord. Amen.

✠ The Blessing of Families

What _____ and _____ do here affects the lives of others almost as profoundly as it affects their own lives. They have families whose relationships will be enlarged and with whom they now embark on a new adventure. We want to include the families and friends as well in our prayers and concern. So let us now pray for them:

O God, who is known in the encounter of person with person, family with family, and tribe with tribe, we magnify your Name for being the One who binds all peoples together. In you, O Lord, shall all the nations of the world be blessed. Our days are as the grass that springs up today and tomorrow is cast into the oven, but your kingdom is forever. Teach us to find wisdom in our human limitations, and thereby to achieve more quickly the lessons of love and understanding.

We pray for these two families being united today, that the ties of relationships being occasioned by this wedding will soon be transcended by a sense of genuine community among them. Let your blessing rest especially on the children, for whom this may seem strange and not a little difficult. May they receive comfort and understanding in their hearts and soon grow into a sense of love and security in their new relationships. Grant that this ceremony and what is accomplished here may lead us all into ever deeper experiences of your grace. Through Jesus Christ our Lord. Amen.

✚ The Preparation

_____, as you stand before the altar of God in the presence of all these people, do you do so with a contrite heart, asking God's forgiveness for all your sins and seeking God's leadership in the new life on which you will now embark?

Bride: I do.

_____, do you also, standing before the altar of God and in the presence of these people, come with a contrite heart, asking God's forgiveness for all your sins and seeking God's leadership in the new life on which you will now embark?

Groom: I do.

✚ The Blessing of the Rings

May I have the rings you intend to give each other? They are beautiful rings. Let us now have a prayer of blessing for them.

Lord, these rings are simple, like your plan for our lives and happiness. They are unbroken in their roundness, like the ages in your sight. They are things of value, like your Word given to us by

110

the prophets of old. Let them become living reminders, we pray, of the simple, unbroken, and valuable love that _____ and _____ have for each other. Grant that nothing may complicate, break, or devalue that love. Teach them, whenever they look on these symbols of affection, to remember this moment, this altar, this company of witnesses, this prayer, and your presence blessing their lives, surrounding them with goodness, and protecting them from evil. Amen.

✚ The Vows with the Exchange of Rings

_____, as you place your ring on _____'s finger and look into her eyes, please repeat after me the words of your sacred vow to her, taken before God and this company:

Groom: I, _____, take you, _____, as my dear and lawful wife. I commit myself to you as your faithful husband, to honor you as a person, to love you as my companion, and to cherish you as a child of God. I intend the love I have for you now to be only the beginning of the love I will come to have as the years go by. I look forward to sharing my life with you, whatever the future holds, and I will comfort you, confide in you, and journey with you from this day forth, whatever the conditions of our lives or of the world around us. So help me, God.

111

_____, as you look into _____'s eyes and place your ring on his finger, please repeat after me the words of your sacred vow to him:

Bride: I, _____, take you _____, as my dear and lawful husband. I commit myself to you as your faithful wife, to honor you as a person, to love you as my companion, and to cherish you as a child of God. I intend the love I have for you now to be only the beginning of the love I will come to have as the years go by. I look forward to sharing my life with you, whatever the future holds, and I will comfort you, confide in you, and journey with you from this day forth, whatever the conditions of our lives or of the world around us. So help me, God.

✠ The Declaration of Union

My friends, this is a joyous moment. By the authority vested in me by the church of Jesus Christ, I now name you husband and wife, joined of God in the presence of all these witnesses. May God enrich you forever through the union you have made and bless your families with the benefits of these new relationships. You may kiss and embrace each other in the joy of what we have done.

✠ The Prayer of Blessing

Now, having begun our celebration in the presence of the One whose holiness is commemorated by this altar, let us conclude by offering prayers of thanksgiving and supplication. Let us pray:

We praise your loving mercy, O God, for the joy and excitement of this blessed occasion. It is you who has given us life and experience and you who has led us to this present moment. We acknowledge and give you thanks for your everlasting care. Cast your mantle of grace and protection on _____ and _____ as they begin this new phase of their journey through life. Safeguard them from perils both seen and unseen. Make them trustworthy to each other and to all whose lives are affected by their marriage. Teach them day by day to love more gently, care more deeply, and share more generously. Let the sun always rise on their good will and let it never set without it. Abide in their home as the One who imparts value to their relationships and meaning to all their efforts. Shelter them from the tragedies so common to human life, or support them that they may stand when visited by adversity. And bring them at last, when life's journey is complete, to rest and repose in our Savior Jesus Christ, to whom be glory forever and ever, world without end, and in whose dear Name we pray:

Congregation: Our Father who art in heaven, Hallowed be your Name. Your kingdom come, your will be done in earth as it is in heaven. Give us this day our

113

daily bread. And forgive us our debts as we forgive our debtors. And lead us not into temptation, but deliver us from evil. For yours is the kingdom, and the power, and the glory for ever. Amen.

From John Killinger, *Contemporary Wedding Services* (Nashville: Abingdon Press, 1986), pp. 39–45. Used by permission.

13

An Ecumenical Ceremony from the Consultation on Common Texts

The congregation stands as the bridal party and ministers enter. Entrance hymn or instrumental music may be used. The people are invited to respond.

✚ Greeting

The grace of our Lord Jesus Christ, the love of God, and the communion of the Holy Spirit be with you all.

Congregation: And also with you.

Dear friends: We have come together in the presence of God. . . . We pray that this couple may fulfill God's purpose for the whole of their lives.

✠ Public Declaration of Intention

The couple declare their intention to marry.

✠ Affirmation by Families and Congregation

Minister: Do you, the families of _____ and _____, give your love and blessing to this new family?

Families: We do.

Minister: Will all of you, by God's grace, do everything in your power to uphold and care for these two persons in their life together?

All: We will.

✠ Prayer of the Day

Minister: Let us pray. . . .

Congregation: Amen.

The congregation is seated.

The Word of God

✠ *First Reading*

The reader may conclude: The Word of the Lord.

Congregation: Thanks be to God.

A psalm or hymn is sung in response to the reading.

✠ *Second Reading*

The reader may conclude: The Word of the Lord.

Congregation: Thanks be to God.

✠ *The Gospel*

An acclamation or hymn may be sung as a preparation for the Gospel.

Before the Gospel, the minister who reads it may say: The Holy Gospel of our Lord Jesus Christ . . .

Congregation: Praise to you, Lord Jesus Christ.

The congregation is seated.

✠ *Sermon or Homily*

A hymn may be sung.

The Marriage

The congregation is seated.

✠ *Marriage Vows*

✠ *Blessing and Exchange of Rings*

Bless, O Lord, (the giving of) these rings . . . through Jesus Christ our Lord.

Congregation: Amen.

✠ *Announcement of the Marriage*

Now that _____ and _____ have given themselves . . . Those whom God has joined together, let no one put asunder.

Congregation: Blessed be the Lord our God now and forever. Amen.

A hymn may be sung.

Prayers

The congregation stands.

✠ *Prayers of Intercession*

The response to the prayers is:

Congregation: We pray to you, our God.

Most gracious God . . .

Congregation: Amen.

118

✚ *Prayer of Blessing*

Blessed are you, Lord God . . .
and glory is yours, Almighty Father, now and forever.

Congregation: Amen.

✚ *Lord's Prayer*

Our Father in heaven,
hallowed be your Name,
your kingdom come,
your will be done,
on earth as in heaven.
Give us today our daily bread.
Forgive us our sins
as we forgive those who sin against us.
Save us from the time of trial
and deliver us from evil.
For the kingdom, the power,
and the glory are yours,
now and forever. Amen.

Conclusion

✚ *Kiss of Peace*

*The Sign of Peace may be exchanged throughout the
congregation.*

119

✠ *Dismissal*

The Lord bless you and keep you . . .

Congregation: Amen.

Go in peace to love and serve the Lord.

Congregation: Thanks be to God.

Concluding hymn, choral, or instrumental music.

From *A Christian Celebration of Marriage: The Consultation on Common Texts* (Philadelphia: Fortress Press, 1987), pp. 28–32. Used by permission.

14

Service of Renewal of Wedding Vows

Couples may request a service of renewal of their wedding vows at the time of a wedding anniversary or following an informal or legal separation. This may occur at a Sunday service or on a separate occasion.

✠ Processional Hymn

✠ Words of Greeting

Dearly beloved, we have gathered together on this special occasion with thanksgiving for God's good gift of Christian marriage. We come to recognize and renew the marriage vows that _____ and _____ have originally taken in (year) _____. We come to ask God's blessing on their marriage as we look to the future.

Holy matrimony was instituted by God, is regulated by his commandments, and was blessed by our Lord Jesus Christ; so it should be held in honor among all people. Let us therefore remember that God has established and set apart marriage for the welfare and happiness of the human family. Therefore our Savior has declared that a man shall leave his father and mother and be joined to his wife, and the two shall become one flesh. In the New Testament our Lord has instructed those who enter marriage to cherish a mutual esteem and love; to share in each other's infirmities and weaknesses; to comfort each other in sickness, trouble, and sorrow; to provide for each other; to pray for and encourage each other; and to live together as heirs of the grace of life.

✚ Scripture Reading

(Select appropriate passages such as Gen. 1:26–28; 2:4–9; 1 Cor. 13:1–13; Eph. 5:21–33, Col. 3:12–17; or 1 John 4:7–16.)

✚ Prayer of Intercession

Heavenly Father, we acknowledge that you have designed the pattern of the family to include marriage that endures through the changes of the years. We thank you for _____ and _____, who celebrate _____ years of married life together. We praise you for the commitment that binds their hearts in Christian love, for the way you have enabled them to keep their vows in all the changing circumstances of life. We ask that you might bless them with continued health. We pray for their children (and grandchildren) that from this example they each might be encouraged to have committed marriages in Christian homes. Use this time of renewal to encourage and strengthen each of us who are here present. May we be given renewed grace to serve you for all the days of our life. This we pray in the Name of Jesus Christ our Creator and Redeemer. Amen.

✚ Renewal of Vows

As the couple face each other, holding hands, they are asked to repeat after the minister the following vows or the ones from their original wedding service.

Man: I, _____, take you, _____, to be my wedded wife. And I promise and covenant anew, before God and these witnesses, to be your loving and faithful husband, in plenty and in want, in joy and in sorrow, in sickness and in health, for as long as we both shall live.

Woman: I, _____, take you, _____, to be my wedded husband. And I promise and covenant anew, before God and these witnesses, to be your loving and faithful wife, in plenty and in want, in joy and in sorrow, in sickness and in health, for as long as we both shall live.

✠ Prayers of Response

By selected family members and/or friends.

✠ Hymn of Thanksgiving

✠ Benediction

The Lord bless you and keep you; the Lord make his face shine upon you and be gracious to you; the Lord turn his face toward you and give you peace. In the Name of the Father, Son, and Holy Spirit. Amen.

PART 3

Resources
for Wedding
Ceremonies

15

Wedding Meditations

Marriage Is Wonderful

D. Stuart Briscoe

Senior Pastor
Elmbrook Church
Waukesha, Wisconsin

Weddings are special. Immaculate tuxedos; pretty dresses; gorgeous flowers; beautiful music; loving friends; happy families; good food; best wishes; high jinks—all this, and a honeymoon, too.

But at the risk of spoiling everything let me remind you that a wedding is not an end in itself. It is a means to an end. It is the start of a marriage.

Our objective today is to launch a marriage! And weddings and marriages should never be confused. They differ dramatically. For one thing, weddings last for half an hour, while marriages are for life. But it's in the practical aspects of life that the differences are seen. Business suits instead of tuxedos; aprons for dresses; bills for flowers; leaky faucets for beautiful music; argumentative neighbors for loving friends; and stomach aches from too much good food—all this, and a mortgage, too.

There's no denying, however, that weddings are fantastic (in the truest sense of the word). They are so beautifully different from everyday life that they border on fantasy. But if weddings are fantastic, marriages are wonderful (in the fullest sense of that word), for they are truly full of wonders. And our task today is not only to enjoy a fantastic wedding but to witness the creation of a wonderful marriage—a thing of wonder.

But what is so wonderful about marriage? I'm glad you asked!

Marriage is wonderful because it was God's idea. Don't believe the modern sociologists who arrogantly claim that marriage is a sociological phenomenon that evolved as humans discovered practical ways of living together, and will eventually and inevitably give place to new and better ways of cohabiting. God, knowing humankind's innate need to love and be loved, from the beginning of creation ordained a relationship in which a man and a woman could learn to meet those divinely imparted deepest needs in each other, and in so doing could discover depths of delight that could come only from the hand of a gracious God. Today you are embarking on an experience of mutual discovery and fulfillment that God longs for you to enjoy and plans for you to experience. This is a thing of wonder.

Marriage is also wonderful because it is initiated in a wedding that God not only attends but in which he actually participates. God gets marriage off on the right foot, in a manner of speaking. He participates in that he "joins two people together." Now I have to admit that I don't know how he does it, but I firmly believe that he does. There is a sense, of course, in which marriage is a legal union. A judge or a sea captain or even a registrar on the strip in Vegas can guarantee that. Strictly speaking, that part of the joining does not require God. But I am talking about something that goes far beyond a legal contract. I'm referring to a union of minds and hearts and spirits and aspirations and longings and dreams and intentions and commitments and resolves. God joins two people together at these intimate levels.

We symbolized this by having the groom enter by one aisle and the bride by the other and inviting you to leave by the same aisle at the same time, preferably hand in hand. In the interim between your individual arrivals and your collective departure God has made himself present in our midst, and in this special place and in a special moment he has joined you together. Don't worry about trying to understand what this means right now, because you have the rest of your lives to explore the significance of what God has done in these last few moments. But whatever you do, don't lose sight of the wonder of it all. At the deepest levels of your existence God has joined you together.

Marriage is wonderful because it is the expression of two people who have been made one. Now usually one plus one equals two. But in divine arithmetic one plus one equals one—a new one, I grant you, but one nevertheless. You've heard men facetiously introduce their wives as their "better half." Whether or not the wife is the "better half" we will not discuss now, but in that both partners are one-half of a new entity they're right! One-half plus one-half equals one. There is a sense in which you are a whole person when you are single but you're only half a married person for the obvious reason it takes two to be married as well as to tango. But when the other half comes along and God joins you together then the two one-halves become one whole. Now if this is getting too mathematical for you, let me give you an illustration from chemistry!

If you take a glass of oxygen—a colorless, odorless gas—and two glasses of hydrogen—another colorless, odorless gas—and pass an electrical current through them, you will probably have an explosion. However, if you do it properly a remarkable thing will happen. The two colorless, odorless gases will become a liquid. Water! H_2O! Now a liquid is totally different from a gas, but if you reverse the process you will find that water is made up of gases. In the same way, at your wedding God has passed his electrical charge through you (didn't you feel it?!) and has taken all that constitutes the bride and all that makes up the groom and fitted them together into a totally new entity. The qualities of both of you will not be lost in this marriage but they will be merged. The weaknesses of neither will evaporate but they will be married to the strengths of the other. In short, the merging and blending of two halves into a new whole is a thing of wonder. When I was married over thirty-five years ago I discovered that I did not stop being me. Neither did Jill stop being she. But together we became something entirely different. She is strong where I am not. Her strength has become part of me. I look at life differently than she does. My perspectives have affected her. We are richer and fuller people because we are a new whole. We are one. Now it didn't always come easily. There were adjustments to be made. New insight requires fresh evaluation. Confronting personal weakness requires courage and demands change. But love finds a way. So don't be misled. A lot of adjustment will be necessary but you have lots of time to do it. Till death do you part, remember?

So thanks for allowing me to share in this fantastic wedding. Now we'll all be watching with great joy the unfolding of your wonderful marriage. Oh, and by the way, don't forget to return the tuxedos. You don't need them for marriage. But in the Lord who made you one, you will find all the resources you need to be all that he intended you to be when he brought you together.

O-Rings and Wedding Rings

Bryan Chapell
Covenant Theological Seminary
St. Louis

> *This is how we know what love is: Jesus Christ laid down his life for us. And we ought to lay down our lives for our brothers. If anyone has material possessions and sees his brother in need but has no pity on him, how can the love of God be in him? Dear children, let us not love with words or tongue but with actions and in truth. (1 John 3:16–18)*

A friend of mine works as an ethno-linguist—he studies cultures through the way they communicate. I know of few careers as interesting as his, but his scientific studies offer little opportunity for wealth and stardom. When we were in grad school together the lack of lucrative potential began to bother him so much that he would lie awake at night plotting how to turn his knowledge into profit. The apparent answer came at a social we attended. Students from throughout the university attended the party. Responding to a friendly challenge about the validity of his studies, my friend claimed that he could pick out the law students attending the party just by listening to their conversation. He succeeded! At the end of the party he had each of the young lawyers fingered.

His success at the party crystallized my friend's plan for profit. He reasoned that since he could identify the speech pattern of lawyers, he should also be able to figure out how really successful lawyers talk. Then for fat fees he would teach this "successful speech" to attorneys hungry for their own career advancement. My friend was sure fame and fortune were right around the corner. His own studies soon convinced him otherwise.

He discovered that young lawyers and law students "sound" like lawyers. The most successful lawyers sound like normal people. The attorneys who really succeed depend on actions, not words.

What is true of law is also true of love: Those whose love succeeds depend on actions, not words. That is really the core of John's message in this text. He writes, "Let us not love with words or tongue but with actions and in truth" (v. 18).

The Problem with Words

We do not have to think long before acknowledging the wisdom of the apostle. We know why words are not enough to secure love. Saying the right words does not secure love. Everyone starts out saying the right words. We all repeat the chorus: "I love you." "This is forever." "I'll never forsake you."

Still, we know saying these right words does not necessarily knit two lives together. The problem is not that people do not mean what they say. People do not lie when they repeat their vows to the preacher. No one plans to have a miserable life. Everyone says, "I love you," and at that moment they mean it. The problem is we can't just depend on words. Words are too slippery.

My wife and I went shopping for a washing machine a couple years ago and discovered how words slip in meaning. We found out that if the capacity of a washer is listed as LARGE, that means "small." If washers are listed as EXTRA LARGE, that means "medium." Only washers with the words SUPER LARGE mean "large." It's even worse if you shop for a mattress. The label FIRM means "soft." The words EXTRA FIRM signify "kinda mushy." SUPER FIRM means "You're gettin' there." You do not find "firm" until you buy what the Sears salesperson calls "Imperial Superba-Firm II."

Words can also have different meanings for different people. For some "forever" means "for a long time." For others "till death do us part" means "until our affections die." In some lives "in sickness and in health" means "as long as you don't make me too miserable, for too long, and it's not your fault."

These differences in meaning are not merely a matter of what we intend to say; they can reflect changes *in* a relationship that change the words *for* that relationship. A woman once told me how the words of her marriage changed as the relationship did. She said, "When I was twenty-one I cried when my husband said 'Good-bye' to go on a business trip because I was so miserable when he was gone. When I was twenty-four I cried when I heard him say 'Hello' because I was so miserable when he was home. Before we were both thirty I stopped crying and he stopped saying 'Hello' or 'Good-bye' because I no longer cared whether he was home or gone."

Whether because words are slippery or because they can change, the result is the same: Words are never enough to seal a love. The problem is not simply that we have such difficulty calibrating "forever" that we really do not know what it means. The real challenge is actually defining love itself. Words cannot adequately express it. The best that words can hardly bear to breathe out still does not say all love must be. What this boils down to is that what we say to each other, or even what we say to ourselves about our feelings for another, still offers no proof of real love.

The Need for Actions

What marks true love if words cannot? The apostle answers that question when he says not to love with lip service but "with actions and in truth" (v. 18).

There is no question about the type of actions John has in mind. He explains in a previous verse where he offers his own definition of love: "This is how we know what love is: Jesus Christ laid down his life for us" (v. 16a).

John defines love by sacrifice. The preeminent example he offers is that of Jesus, who willingly gave up his glory and privileges to suffer on the cross for your good and mine. John goes on to say that "we ought to lay down our lives" for each other (v. 16b), and offers the concrete example of sharing our material possessions with those in need as embodying this type of love (v. 17).

No mystery lies in applying these truths to marriage. The love that secures this relationship must also be sacrificial. This does not mean that God expects you to die physically for each other every day. It does mean that you are to die to self each day. The satisfaction of your own needs and desires cannot be the primary reason you enter this relationship. Such motives will never allow true love to grow.

In Christian marriage each individual's actions have an *other* focus. Manipulation, intimidation, and deceit for personal gain have no place here. Such actions will destroy true love even if they secure personal advantages for a time. The Bible here simply puts before us the wonderful mystery of human happiness that in the giving of self lies life's greatest gains. The greatest love grows where self is served the least. This mystery takes concrete form in our marriages when we patiently endure one another's fears and foolishness, refuse to take advantage of another's weaknesses or our own strengths, submit to one another's needs, and forgive one another's sins.

The Truths That Count

These last words about forgiveness are important for they remind us that all these instructions *sound* great until we disappoint, frustrate, or sin against one another. Then loving actions become enormous challenges. Not only do we have trouble forgiving; the very fact that we find this divine imperative a struggle reveals the spiritual weakness in each of our own hearts. That is why the apostle John told us we had to love "in truth" as well as in deed. That "truth" involves more than dealing with one another in integrity. Each of us must also face a vital truth about ourselves: We are far less capable of real love than we readily dare to confess. What the apostle has told us to *be* in our marriages is *beyond* us. It is beyond us all never to manipulate, intimidate, or take advantage.

This truth is most evident when we consider *why* Christ died. John tells us about the sacrifice of Jesus not merely to give us an example to mimic, but to remind us of our guilt that he must cover. Yet in this reminder there is more than the exposure of truth about ourselves; there is the revelation of a God who is *for* us.

In the sacrifice of his Son our God reveals his desire to bless us. Not only does he offer us forgiveness for our own sins, but as we humbly contemplate the love that he shed for us we find the willingness to share it with another. In recognition of our own need for forgiveness we discover the heart to forgive that heals and seals our relationships. This is why love has a chance despite the truth of personal sinfulness we each must confess.

As wonderful as it is to discover and share the truths of our Savior's forgiveness, this is not the end of our blessing. As we revel in our Savior's love and honor him with our lives, something else very special happens. Perhaps I can picture this added truth for you by reminding you of a game you may have played. The version of this game my family owns includes a steel ball and two steel rods placed so as to create a small incline. The goal of the game is to make the ball climb uphill by applying just the right pressure to the rods. Something else automatically happens as the ball rises: The higher the rods lift the ball, the closer together they come. When two lives in a marriage honor the Lord, the same dynamics occur: The higher we lift him, the closer together we grow.

The truths reflected in this game should remind you that commitments you make today are not merely between the two of you. When you vow to love and honor one another you also make these promises *before* and *to* your God. As you commit your lives to honoring him, you invite his care to bring you closer each day. You need never be like those persons who look back on their wedding day or their first days together as the best time of their marriages. As your lives acknowledge him, your love only gets better and better. Think of how wonderful is this blessing. As happy as you are now, this is only the beginning of the joy you will know as you continue to serve the Lord with your lives.

Though words may fail, actions motivated by these truths your hearts confess will mold your love into the marriage you most desire. Your spiritual commitments—what is deepest in your hearts rather than outward words or deeds—ultimately will secure what is dearest in your lives.

We should not be surprised that what's inside is so important. When the tragedy of the *Challenger* space shuttle shook our nation, investigators went to amazing lengths to discern the cause. Do you remember what they found? In the cold temperatures the O-Rings around the engines failed, causing a fuel leak that ignited. Initially this analysis surprised some at NASA because inspectors had externally examined the O-Rings just prior to the flight. Everything looked fine on the outside. What the disaster investigation revealed was that no external inspection was meaningful because what happened was due to failures on the inside of those rings.

Now the two of you assume the wearing of wedding "O-Rings." The words that you say and these bands you wear make everything appear fine on the outside. Remember, what's inside counts even more. In the actions and acknowledgments of the heart reside the spiritual commitments that will make your words and actions truly and eternally loving. May the Lord make your lives as sweet as he desires by drawing your hearts together in love for him.

Closer to God, Closer to Each Other

John Guest

Episcopalian Minister
The John Guest Evangelistic Team

What does God want for your marriage? The answer is simple: God wants your marriage to be filled with joy! That's why he created us in his image, as male and female, so that we might be fulfilling to one another; as Jesus said, "These things I say to you, that my joy may be in you, and that your joy may be full" (John 15:11).

God is a joyful Person! He's not some sanctified, sterile, white-tiled emergency room, which smells of antiseptic. That's not a very joyful image. God is not sterile; God's holiness isn't sterility. God is full of joy. And Jesus said, "These things I say to you, that *my* joy may be in you." Jesus was a joyful Person. He wasn't a drab, long-faced person.

You are never going to know joy like God wants you to experience unless you're prepared to come out into the open, unless you're prepared to get your priorities straight, unless you're prepared to give him time and energy and pay the cost involved. Do you want a joyful marriage? Do you want it to be terrific? Get out into the open with God. It's when you get out into the open with God and walk out into the open with him that you are going to have the power to become vulnerable with one another.

Most of us are not willing to become vulnerable. I've discovered in my counseling that most people take the area that's very painful in their lives to their partner, and put a wall around it. Every time their partner steps over that fence, into that area of their lives, they explode or go crazy in some way. Some just explode and control that fence with anger. Some just make a little quip about it, using little funny lines to cover it up. Some may sulk. I used to be an incredible sulker and a very painful person to live with.

If you have a little piece of your life and you are protecting it by saying or thinking, "Look, I'm not prepared to deal with this. I don't want this out in the open. You aren't going to touch this or change it," whenever that piece of your life is violated by your partner, you've got to get that piece out into the open before God and allow him to help you deal with it. It's only as you do that with him that you're going to be able to take that last frontier of your life—or frontiers if you have three or four such little pieces of space—and deal with it.

You don't have to be married very long to find out what some of those fences are in your relationship. There are land mines just on the other side of them! And when you step on a land mine, it has a certain given effect! And when you get hit with those effects long enough, you say "Enough of that! I'm not getting in that piece of space ever again with her (him)! It's going to destroy our marriage!"

We've got to go to God with those issues first. If you can't take it to God then you're never going to put it straight with each other. Because *when we get closer to God we get closer to each other.*

One evening as my wife and I were contemplating all the wonderful things of which we are deeply appreciative, she said that there is nothing like the joy of being close to Jesus. A nice home or vacation doesn't even begin to touch it. Being close to Jesus transforms all those other things—the home, the job, the family, and *your marriage.*

To enjoy this relationship with Christ, as well as the growing relationship with your spouse, there are practical steps you need to take.

First, you've got to get down on your knees and pray. You may ask, "Why on my knees?" Well, no casual posture is a fitting preparation for serious conversation with God. What you do with your body communicates what you think of what you are doing. When you get down on your knees, there is nothing else you are getting on your knees to do but pray. When you get down on your knees and see yourself before God, you will be putting yourself in an attitude of prayer. You will be preparing the way to pray.

Second, get your head seriously into the Word of God. There is no short-cut. This is not a clever little how-to. It is a how-to but a costly how-to. You are going to have to carve out time, not just to be with God in prayer, but to get into his Word.

Third, allow your home to be a place of ministry. When you intentionally, not casually, take your family and home and open it up for ministry, the Lord will use it in a great way. Your family and home can be a tremendous example of the love you have for God, as well as the love you have for each other. Even if you don't think you are all you should be, make the benchmark, openly commit to it, and then fill in the space between the benchmark and where you are. God will honor it.

These three practical steps for communing with God will help you and your spouse to both grow in love and respect for God, and in love and respect for each other as well.

Wedding Gifts (1 Corinthians 13)

David W. Wiersbe

Senior Pastor
Hope Evangelical Free Church
Roscoe, Illinois

Mike and Kathy, the day we've planned for is finally here! All the preparation and last-minute details are done. It's time to say those important words that will launch you into life's greatest adventure. Your family and friends are here, watching and wishing you well. And they've brought gifts. I saw a table piled high with beautifully wrapped presents in the fellowship hall.

Certainly gifts are appropriate. Every bride and groom needs help getting started. The gifts you'll receive, Kathy and Mike, are expressions of love from your family and friends. Let's be honest: We like to get gifts! But the most important gifts being given today aren't on the table in the fellowship hall. They are right here in this room.

You are here this afternoon, ready to pledge yourselves to each other, because of love. *The love you share is a gift from God.* You remember well the first time you met. Kathy wasn't too impressed with you, Mike! But over time you got to know each other, and dislike turned into "like," and now like has grown into love.

The love that has grown deep and strong is a precious gift, and it comes from the God who brought you two together. It was no accident that the two of you met at camp that summer. It was divine appointment. So the gift of love that brings you to be married is something to be treasured.

The love God causes to grow between a man and a woman needs to be nurtured. Think of love as a seed. It must be planted in good soil, in hearts that are tender. It has to be watered with words of affection, with deeds of kindness. In the right environment, the seed of love puts down deep roots, produces beautiful foliage, and bears the fruit of joy and peace and grace. Where real love is, others want to be. And so we are all here, rejoicing at the beautiful relationship that you two enjoy.

In taking your vows today, Mike and Kathy, you are making a covenant. As we've talked together about marriage, you've come to understand that the love you share is for a lifetime. Today we celebrate this precious gift from God, the love that you two share.

There is another gift being given today. *You are each God's gift to the other.* The Scripture tells us that it isn't good for a man or a woman to be alone. So God makes each of us a helpmate, a man or woman who will complete us, who will make us strong where we're weak.

Mike, look at Kathy. What a beautiful bride— your bride. She is God's unique gift to you. There's no other woman in the world with her blend of beauty, graces, and gifts. As she's grown up, God has been preparing her to be your wife. So, Mike, *never* take this beautiful woman for granted. She is your partner, your lover, your best friend. She is God's gift to you. She's the only woman you'll ever need!

Kathy, look at Mike. Looks good in a tux, right? Kathy, Mike is the man God has prepared to be your husband. He will be able to meet your needs, encourage you to pursue your dreams, be with you through life's storms and in life's moments of greatness. Don't ever allow yourself to think of Mike as "him." He is God's special gift to you, Kathy, for your very own.

One more gift must be mentioned, although it's a gift you've each had for some time. *Jesus is God's best gift to you.* "For God so loved the world, that he gave his only-begotten Son . . ." Giving is an evidence of love. When you love, you have to give.

That's true of God. He loves each one of us, in spite of our sins and our failures. To deal with the problem of our sin, he gave a gift, and no ordinary or cheap gift: He gave us his very best, his own Son.

Because Jesus died for our sins and then rose from the dead, we can be confident about where we'll be when it comes our time to die. And when you're sure about your destination, you can enjoy the journey. Both Mike and Kathy have a personal relationship to Jesus Christ. They have trusted him as their Savior, and they want him to be the Lord of their lives and new home.

Jesus is God's best gift because he meets our deepest needs—our need for forgiveness, for direction in life, for the resources it takes to live with integrity and have a godly home. Jesus is God's best gift because he can't be lost or taken away. When he comes into your life, he's there to stay! And so a marriage is not a union of two lives; it's a dance with three partners: Mike, Kathy, and the Lord Jesus. And, as the Scriptures say, "A cord of three strands is not easily broken" (Eccles. 4:12).

Now, a few words to the parents of the bride and groom. Mr. and Mrs. Smith, Mr. and Mrs. Johnson, I commend you for the way you reared your children. As parents you've modeled the kind of love I've been talking about. That's clear from the way Kathy and Mike treat each other. You should be proud of what you've accomplished. You've transmitted your faith, and your values. In a few minutes, your children will officially be leaving home. But you're not losing your children. In fact, you're each gaining a delightful new family member (and an extra person to buy presents for!). But this is as it should be. May God bless you for your faithfulness as parents, and as models of Christian marriage.

The commitment and emotion that bind you together, Mike and Kathy, are God's gift of love. As you undergo the transformation from bride and groom to wife and husband, you are each God's gift to the other. And always, God's best gift to you is Jesus. As long as you treasure these gifts, protect and celebrate them, you will be the world's most "gifted" people.

16

Lighting of a Unity Candle

✤ *At an appropriate point in the ceremony, after the exchange of vows, a candle-lighting ceremony may be included. Generally a three-candle candelabra is employed. The outer two candles are lit in advance. This may occur during the prelude prior to the ceremony. A groomsman or the parents of the bride or groom may be asked to light these two candles. At the appointed time in the ceremony the minister may say:*

✤ _____ and _____, you have exchanged vows and rings expressing your desire to be united as one in a Christ-honoring marriage. Jesus Christ, who caused light to shine out of darkness at the beginning of creation, also made this claim: "I am the light of the world. Whoever follows me will never walk in darkness, but will have the light of life. You are the light of the world. Let your light so shine before men, that they may see your good deeds and praise your Father in heaven."

As you enter marriage may the light of his presence in your life and his works through you be seen as a light in the darkness. May that truth be reflected as you now take the flames from two separate candles and blend them into the one center candle. May the Lord unite you with one faith, one hope, and one love. May you, _____ and _____, be one in name, one in aim, and one in commitment to the one and only true God, Father, Son, and Holy Spirit. Amen.

✤ *Following the lighting of the center candle and the extinguishing of the two side candles, the couple may return to a kneeling bench in front of the minister, at which time he may lead them in a prayer of dedication.*

✤ *An alternate arrangement is to have the bride's parents come to the platform and light the candle on the bride's side of the candelabra. The groom's parents come and then light the candle on the groom's side. The bride and groom then step to the candelabra, withdraw their respective candle from the candelabra, and jointly light the center candle. Then they extinguish their separate candles and replace them in the holder.*

17

The Lord's Supper at a Wedding

Communion for Bride and Groom

✤ As husband and wife, _____ and _____ desire to honor and obey Christ their Lord in all aspects of their marriage. In obedience to his command to "Do this in remembrance of me," they desire to partake of the Lord's Supper. Having both exercised saving faith in Christ, they now receive the bread and cup as indicated in these words of Scripture:

✤ "I received from the Lord what I also passed on to you: the Lord Jesus, on the night he was betrayed, took bread, and when he had given thanks, he broke it and said, 'This is my body, which is for you; do this in remembrance of me'" (1 Cor. 11:23–24).

Let us pray . . .

The minister then passes the bread to the bride and groom, who partake.

✠ Scripture also says, "In the same way, after supper he took the cup, saying 'This cup is the new covenant in my blood; do this, whenever you drink it, in remembrance of me.' For whenever you eat this bread and drink this cup, you proclaim the Lord's death until he comes" (1 Cor. 11:25–26).

The minister then passes the cup to the bride and groom, who partake.

✠ *This may be followed by a hymn, prayer, or benediction.*

Communion for Congregation

✠ *Words of Institution*

Hear now the words of institution of the Lord's Supper that Christ, the Groom, intends for us, his bride: *Read 1 Corinthians 11:23–29.*

✠ *Words of Invitation*

Christ invites all those who repent of their sins, who place their faith in his person and saving work on the cross, and who remain in the fellowship of his church, to come to his table. We do so looking back with thanksgiving for his atoning death on the cross to forgive our sins, as well as looking forward with anticipation to his promised return for his bride so we can celebrate together at the wedding supper of the Lamb. So we invite all who know Christ and are part of his church to participate with us in his presence.

✛ *Prayer of Confession and Thanksgiving*

✛ *Receiving of the Bread*

(The elements may be passed to the guests in their pews or the guests may be asked to come forward to receive both elements.)

Take and eat, remembering and believing that the body of Christ was broken for us, his bride, to provide complete forgiveness of all our sins.

✛ *Receiving of the Cup*

Take and eat, remembering and believing, that the blood of Christ was shed for us, his bride, to provide complete forgiveness of all our sins.

✛ *Scripture Reading*

Listen now to the words of Scripture:

"The twenty-four elders and the four living creatures fell down and worshipped God, who was seated on the throne. And they cried, 'Amen, Hallelujah!' Then a voice came from the throne saying, 'Praise our God, all you his servants, you who fear him, both small and great!' Then I heard what sounded like a great multitude, like the roar of rushing waters and like loud peals of thunder, shouting, 'Hallelujah! For the Lord God Almighty reigns. Let us rejoice and be glad and give him glory! For the wedding of the Lamb has come, and his bride has made herself ready. Fine linen, bright and clean, was given her to wear.' Then the angel said to me, 'Write: Blessed are those who are invited to the wedding supper of the Lamb! And he added, These are the true words of God'" (Rev. 19:4–9). Amen.

✣ Hymn or Benediction

18

Alternate Wedding Vows

✥ _____, I take you to be my wife/husband from this time forward, to join with you and to share all that the Lord has planned for us, to give and to receive from his hand, to speak and to listen, to inspire and to respond, and in all the circumstances of our married life to be faithful to you with my life and with all my being for as long as we both shall live.

✥ *Groom:* _____, I love you as Christ loves us, unconditionally, unselfishly, and eternally. In the presence of God, our family, and friends, I receive you as my wife and helpmeet, a gift from the Lord. Using Scripture as my guide, I promise to be the head and spiritual leader of our home, to protect and provide for you. I commit myself to do these things through the power of God's Holy Spirit for as long as we live.

Bride: _____, I love you as Christ loves us, unconditionally, unselfishly, and eternally. In the presence of God, our family, and friends, I receive you as my husband, a gift from God. I will accept your spiritual headship and promise to honor, respect, exhort, trust, and provide a loving home for you. I commit myself to do these things through the power of God's Holy Spirit for as long as we live.

✤ *Groom:* I, _____, take you, _____, just as you are, to share the whole of my life as my wife in a Christian marriage. I promise to love you even as Christ loved the church and gave himself for her. With God's help, I will love and cherish you at all times, in all circumstances. I will value and respect you for the person you are and the wife you will be to me. I promise to provide the necessary leadership to establish our home under the Lordship of Christ as we serve him together to the glory of God.

Bride: I, _____, take you, _____, just as you are, to share the whole of my life as my husband in a Christian marriage. I promise to love and respect you, even as the church is subject to Christ, her Lord. With God's help, I will love you at all times and in all circumstances. I will value and respect you for the person you are and the husband you will be to me. I promise to work with you to establish our home under the Lordship of Christ as we serve him together to the glory of God.

✠ _____ and _____, you have come to express publicly your desire to be formally united in the covenant bonds of a Christian marriage. Therefore I ask you to now join hands, remembering that the closer you keep Christ at the center of your life, the greater can be your closeness to one another.

_____, in taking _____ to be your lawfully wedded wife/husband, before God and these witnesses, do you promise to love her/him, to honor and cherish her/him, and, forsaking all others, to cling only to her/him as a faithful husband/wife so long as you both shall live? If this expresses your intention and promise, answer "I do, with the Lord's strength and help."

✠ _____, I take you now to be my husband/wife. I promise to live with you, to trust you, and to be faithful to you. I will love you when we are apart as well as when we are together. I will love you in sickness and in health, in the joyful as well as the sad times of life. I will work with you toward our common goals in order that Christ might be honored in our relationship and in our home. I pledge myself to be faithful to you with my body, my mind, and my heart, for our whole life, so help me God.

19

Suggested Scripture Readings for Weddings

✙ Suggested Old Testament Readings

Genesis 1:26–28
Genesis 2:4–9, 15–24
Psalm 22:25–31
Psalm 37:3–6
Psalm 127
Psalm 128
Song of Solomon 2:10–13; 8:6–7
Isaiah 43:1–7
Isaiah 55:10–13
Isaiah 61:1–3, 10–11
Isaiah 61:10–62:3

✢ Suggested New Testament Readings

Matthew 5:1–10, 13–16
Matthew 7:21, 24–29
Matthew 19:4–6
Matthew 22:35–40
Mark 2:18–22
Mark 10:6–9, 13–16
John 2:1–10
John 15:8–17
1 Corinthians 13:1–13
Ephesians 3:14–21
Ephesians 5:1–2, 21–33
Colossians 3:12–17
1 John 4:7–16
Revelation 19:4–9

20

Wedding Prayers

✠ Eternal God, creator and preserver of all life, author of salvation, and giver of all grace, look with favor upon the world you have made, and for which your Son gave his life, and especially upon this man and this woman whom you made one flesh in holy matrimony. Amen.

Give them wisdom and devotion in the ordering of their common life, that each may be to the other a strength in need, a counselor in perplexity, a comfort in sorrow, and a companion in joy. Amen.

Grant that their wills may be so knit together in your will and their spirits in your Spirit, that they may grow in love and peace with you and one another all the days of their life. Amen.

Give them grace, when they hurt each other, to recognize and acknowledge their fault, and to seek each other's forgiveness and yours. Amen.

Make their life together a sign of Christ's love to this sinful and broken world, that unity may overcome estrangement, forgiveness heal guilt, and joy conquer despair. Amen.

Bestow on them, if it is your will, the gift and heritage of children, and the grace to bring them up to know you, to love you, and to serve you. Amen.*

✠ Almighty Father, whose presence is the source of every happiness, we pray that you will be present to grant your blessings on this man and woman. May they be truly joined in holy marriage according to your covenant. In your good providence you have brought them together for this moment. Grant them the frame of heart to enter this new relationship. Equip them with your grace, so they can enjoy the comforts, cares, trials, and duties of life together in a way that honors your Name. Please guide and protect them from this day forward as long as they both shall live. This we pray in the Name of our Lord and Savior Jesus Christ. Amen.

---

*From *The Book of Common Prayer* (The Church Hymnal Corporation and The Seabury Press, 1979), p. 429. Used by permission.

✠ Lord God, our Redeemer and the Creator of marriage, bless this couple as they come in the presence of family and friends to affirm the choice they have made to accept each other as life companions. Confirm within both of them a desire to establish a home in which your love and presence may be celebrated freely. Deliver them from empty words and shallow commitments. May your Word nurture them all the days of their lives as they attempt to discover and fulfill your will. May they find in their family, friends, and the church community both examples and encouragement to keep the vows they made and to continue to grow in their walk with you. Hear these petitions we pray, with faith in Jesus Christ our Lord. Amen.

✠ Our Father, life is full of your grace and beauty, and we are grateful for the eyes to behold this. Yet it is also often a struggle, a pilgrimage in which we learn things we wish we had known in the beginning. We pray for _____ and _____ as they begin their journey. Teach them how to share so intimately all their thoughts, hopes, and fears that each will take courage from the other and learn to deal more confidently with himself or herself and with life. Let them learn quickly how to express love within the marriage relationship, that in expressing it they may also discover how to love better. Grant that they may be accepting and forgiving of each other's faults and shortcomings, that each may more readily deal with his or her inner problems in such a supportive atmosphere. Teach them patience and kindness, and excitement in each other's differences, that they may see themselves complemented and enriched, each in the other, instead of threatened or challenged by diversity. If it is your will to bless them with children, grant them strength, wisdom, and tolerance to be helpful, caring parents. Give them a sense of humor about themselves and their relationship, that they may keep their smaller differences and misunderstandings in true perspective.

Bless their larger families with the grace to be good relations, who prove supportive in times of need and loving and encouraging at all other times as well. And, above all and in all, grant them a steady awareness of your loving presence, that they may live with the assurance of the meaning of their relationship and existence, knowing that what we have now sealed here is guaranteed by the Name that is above every name, even Jesus Christ our Lord, who has taught us to pray, saying, Our Father . . .*

---

*From John Killinger, *Contemporary Wedding Services* (Nashville: Abingdon Press, 1986), pp. 17–18. Used by permission.

✥ Unison by Congregation

Most gracious God, we give you thanks for your unmerited love in sending Jesus Christ to come among us. We thank you for consecrating the union of man and woman in Christian marriage, which you have created. By the power of your Holy Spirit, pour out the abundance of your blessings on _____ and _____. Grant them the grace and strength always to remain faithful to the covenant that they have made in your presence and before us, their family and friends. Let their love for each other be a seal on their hearts, a mantle about their shoulders, and a crown on their foreheads.

Bless them in their work and in their companionship; in their waking and sleeping; in their joys and their sorrows; in life and in death. May Jesus Christ be the center of their relationship. May his presence be evident to all who enter their home. This we pray through Christ Jesus our Lord, who with you and the Holy Spirit lives and reigns, one God, forever and ever. Amen.

21

Wedding Music

✥ Preludes

J. S. Bach, If Thou Be Near

J. S. Bach, Jesu, Joy of Man's Desiring

J. S. Bach, Let All Together Praise Our God

J. S. Bach, Rejoice, Ye Christians

J. S. Bach, Sheep May Safely Graze

J. S. Bach, Now Thank We All Our God (Cantata No. 79)

Dietrich Buxtehude, Prelude and Fugue in E

David Cherwien, "Interpretations" based on Hymn Tunes

John Cook, Fanfare (can also be used as recessional)

Emma Lou Diemer, Rejoice, Ye Pure in Heart

Theodore duBois, Cantilena Nuptiale

George Frederick Handel, Adagio movements from "Six Sonatas for Violin"

Joseph Jongen, Choral

Sigfrid Karg-Elert, Choral Improvisations—selected

C. S. Lang, Tuba Tune in D Major

Paul Manz, Choral Improvisations—selected

Gilbert Martin, Laudation

Felix Mendelssohn, excerpts from Organ Sonatas

Johann Pachelbel, Prelude on Old One Hundredth

Henry Purcell, Voluntary on Old One Hundredth

John Stanley, A Trumpet Tune for Flutes

John Stanley, Toccata for the Flutes

Albert Travis, Let All Mortal Flesh Keep Silence

Gordon Young, Prelude in Classic Style

✥ Processionals

J. S. Bach, Sinfonia from Wedding Cantata, 196

Marcus Enrico Bossi, The Wedding March, opus 110

André Campra, Rigaudon

Garry A. Cornell, Joyous Procession

William Croft, Voluntary in C

Raymond Haan, Ceremonial Trumpet Tune

George Frederick Handel, Aria in F Major

George Frederick Handel, Larghetto in F

George Frederick Handel, Processional in G Major

George Frederick Handel, Water Music

David N. Johnson, Processional in E Flat

Henry Purcell, Trumpet Tunes

Henry Purcell, Trumpet Voluntary (Prince of Denmark's March)

Raymond Sonderlund, Fanfare March

Louis Vierne, Nuptial March, opus 51, no. 6

Robert Wetzler, Processional on "Westminster Abbey"

✛ Vocal Music

J. S. Bach, Be Thou with Them

J. S. Bach, Jesu, Joy of Man's Desiring

J. S. Bach, Jesus, Shepherd, Be Thou Near Me

J. S. Bach, My Heart Ever Faithful

J. S. Bach, O Love That Casts Out Fear

Leonard Bernstein, A Simple Song

Roberta Bitgood, The Greatest of These Is Love

Johannes Brahms, Though I Speak

Brother James' Air

Scott Wesley Brown, I Wish You Jesus

Scott Wesley Brown, My Treasure (A Wedding Song)

Scott Wesley Brown, This Is the Way (A Wedding Song)

Fern Glasgow Dunlap, Wedding Prayer

Antonin Dvorak, Biblical Songs

Tina English, And On This Day

Don Francisco, I Could Never Promise You

Cesar Franck, O Lord Most Holy

Charles Francois Gounod, Entreat Me Not to Leave

George Frederick Handel, Thanks Be to Thee

George Frederick Handel, Wedding Hymn

Richard K. Lindroth, Our Wedding Song

Austin C. Lovelace, O God of Love, To Thee We Bow

Austin C. Lovelace, O Saviour, Guest Most Bounteous

Austin C. Lovelace, A Wedding Blessing

Daniel Moe, The Greatest of These Is Love

Flor Peeters, Wedding Song

Mary Rice, Wedding Prayer

Heinrich Schuetz, Wedding Song

Robert Schumann, The Ring

Ralph Vaughan Williams, The Call

Edward H. Wetherill, A Marriage Prayer

✤ Congregational Hymns

Children of the Heavenly Father

For the Beauty of the Earth

I with Thee Would Begin

Joyful, Joyful, We Adore Thee

Lord, Today Bless This New Marriage

Love Divine, All Loves Excelling

Now Thank We All Our God

O Jesus, Joy of Loving Hearts

O Perfect Love

Praise to the Lord, the Almighty

Savior, Like a Shepherd Lead Us

We Praise You, O God

✛ Recessionals

J. S. Bach, In Thee Is Gladness

John Behnke, Prelude on "All Creatures of Our God and King"

Leon Boellmann, Chorale (Suite Gothique)

George Frederick Handel, Allegro Maestoso (Water Music)

George Frederick Handel, March from "Occasional Oratorio"

George Frederick Handel, Postlude in G

Benedetto Marcello, Psalm XIX

Gilbert Martin, Dialogue

Johann Pachelbel, Chromatic Fugue

Henry Purcell, Trumpet Tunes

John Stanley, Trumpet Voluntary

Charles Widor, Toccata (Symphony 5)

Healey Willan, Gelobt Sei Gott

22

Planning Charts

Request for a Wedding

	Bride	Groom
Full name		
Address		
Home phone		
Work phone		
Church member- ship		
Parents' names		

Parents' phone

Parents' address

Grandparents or other relatives for special seating:

_____

_____

_____

Future address of bride and groom: _____

_____

Minister to conduct ceremony: _____

_____

Other clergy to assist: _____

Has either of you been married before? _____

Rehearsal: Date_____ Time _____

Wedding: Date _____ Time _____

Members of wedding party:

Name   Role

Resources for Wedding Ceremonies

Who have you enlisted for the following:

	Name	Phone
Organist		
Vocalist(s)		
Other musicians		
Florist		
Wedding hostess		
Photographer		
Videographer		

Any others assisting in the wedding:

Name	Role

Where would you like to have the receiving line?

_____

Who would you like to be included? _____

_____

_____

_____

✛ Ceremony Preferences

What music would you like to have included (vocal, instrumental, congregational singing)? _____

_____

_____

Rings: Single_____ Double_____

Resources for Wedding Ceremonies

Do you have any preferences for Scripture readings?

_____

_____

_____

Do you prefer to memorize your vows or repeat them after the minister? _____

_____

Do you want to have a unity candle lighting?_____

Do you plan to have a kneeling bench?_____

Any other preferences to be considered in planning the ceremony?

_____

_____

_____

When do you plan to have photographs taken of the wedding party?

_____

_____

Location of reception: _____

Time: _____

Minister's Wedding Ceremony Planning Sheet

	Bride	Groom
Full name		
Home phone		
Work phone		

Date and time of wedding: _____

Date and time of rehearsal: _____

	Name	Phone
Other clergy assisting		
Organist		
Vocalists		

Other instrumen-talists		

Prelude Time

Scheduled times of arrival of members of wedding party: _____

_____

_____

Time for prelude to begin: _____

Music to include: _____

_____

Seating:

	When	Ushered by
Groom's grand-mother		
Groom's grand-father		
Bride's grand-mother		
Bride's grandfather		
Groom's mother		
Groom's father		

Bride's mother		
Others		

Candle lighting:

Who	When	Where

Runner down center aisle: _____

Processional

Musical cue: _____

Order of party in procession:

Name	Role

Resources for Wedding Ceremonies

Ceremony

Item	Directions
Vocal music	
Instrumental music	
Scripture readings	
Giving away of bride	
Vows (memorized? special requests?)	
Rings	
Kneeling	
Unity candle	

Communion	
Meditation	
Introduction of bride and groom	
Other	

Any unusual requests or factors to keep in mind:

_____

_____

Recessional

Any unusual instructions: _____

_____

_____

Order of recessional: _____

_____

_____

Arrangements for ushering people out: _____

_____

_____

Receiving line: _____

_____

_____

Processional and Recessional Diagrams

Processional

From front of sanctuary:

① Minister

② Groom

③ Best man

④ Groomsmen/Ushers

From back of sanctuary:

① Bridesmaids

② Maid/matron of honor

③ Flower girl

④ Ring-bearer

⑤ Bride on her father's right arm (Mother of bride stands as they enter)

Front of church sanctuary

Minister

Bride   Groom

Father
of Bride

| Bridesmaids | Flower Girl | Maid of Honor | Best Man | Ring Bearer | Groomsmen |

Bride's parents	Groom's parents
Bride's relatives	Groom's relatives
Guests	Guests

Recessional

① Bride and groom

② Flower girl and ring-bearer

③ Maid/matron of honor and best man

④ Groomsmen and bridesmaids

⑤ Minister

Also by Paul E. Engle

Baker's Funeral Handbook: Resources for Pastors
*Baker's Worship Handbook: Traditional and
    Contemporary Service Resources*
Discovering the Fullness of Worship
*The Governor Drove Us Up the Wall: A Guide
    to Nehemiah*
Guarding and Growing: A Study in 2 Peter
Worship Planbook: A Manual for Worship Leaders